D0706647

Punctuation Matters

Punctuation Matters gives straight answers to the queries raised most frequently by practitioners in computing, engineering, medicine, and science as they grapple with day-to-day tasks in writing and editing. The advice it offers is based on John Kirkman's long experience of providing courses on writing and editing in academic centres, large companies, research organisations, and government departments, in the UK, Europe, and in the USA. Sample material discussed in the book comes from real documents from computing, engineering, and scientific contexts, giving the guidelines an immediately recognisable, 'true to life' relevance. The advice is down-to-earth and up-to-date.

The book is clearly set out in three parts:

- Part 1 states a policy for clear and reliable punctuation;

- Part 2 gives a series of alphabetically arranged guidelines, to be 'dipped into' for guidance on how to use the main punctuation marks in English;

- Part 3 contains appendices on paragraphing, word-division, and how conventions of punctuation differ in the UK and the USA.

Punctuation Matters is the essential guide for everyone who has to write in scientific, technical and medical contexts, with clear explanations on punctuation, what it does, and how to use it.

John Kirkman is a consultant on scientific and technical communication.

Punctuation Matters

Advice on punctuation
for scientific and technical
writing

Fourth edition

John Kirkman

 Routledge
Taylor & Francis Group

LONDON AND NEW YORK

First published as Full Marks 1989, 1993, 1999 by Ramsbury Books
This fourth edition 2006 by Routledge
2 Park Square, Milton Park, Abingdon, Oxon OX14 4RN

Simultaneously published in the USA and Canada
by Routledge
270 Madison Ave, New York, NY 10016

Routledge is an imprint of the Taylor & Francis Group, an informa business

© 1989, 1993, 1999, 2006 John Kirkman

Typeset in Garamond by Keystroke, 28 High Street, Tettenhall, Wolverhampton
Printed and bound in Great Britain by TJ International Ltd, Padstow, Cornwall

All rights reserved. No part of this book may be reprinted or reproduced
or utilised in any form or by any electronic, mechanical, or other means,
now known or hereafter invented, including photocopying and recording,
or in any information storage or retrieval system, without permission in
writing from the publishers.

British Library Cataloguing in Publication Data
A catalogue record for this book is available from the British Library

Library of Congress Cataloging in Publication Data
A catalog record has been requested for this book

ISBN10: 0–415–39981–5 (hbk)
ISBN10: 0–415–39982–3 (pbk)

ISBN13: 978–0–415–39981–4 (hbk)
ISBN13: 978–0–415–39982–1 (pbk)

Contents

Preface

How to use this book

This book is in three parts: Part 1 is a statement of policy; Part 2 is a set of guidelines; Part 3 contains two appendices on topics closely allied to punctuation, and an appendix on conventions of punctuation in the USA.

If possible, read Part 1 at a single sitting. It is a discussion, setting out the reasoning behind my approach to punctuation.

Do *not* try to read Part 2 as a continuous discussion. It is a series of guidelines, arranged alphabetically, designed to be 'dipped into' when you want guidance on how to use the main punctuation marks in English. The Contents list will direct you to the main sections, and the Index will help you find the topic that interests you.

Part 3 is also designed to be 'dipped into' when you want guidance. Appendix 1 discusses paragraphing, and Appendix 2 discusses word-division. These topics are not strictly aspects of punctuation. However, they are closely related to punctuation because they are additional means of showing up your meaning on a printed page, so I have included a brief discussion of them as appendices in this book.

I have also included in Part 3 an appendix describing the ways in which conventions of punctuation in American English differ from the conventions in British English. Many writers and editors who normally work in British English have to produce drafts of texts for publication in the USA or for publication world-wide on behalf of American companies. It is therefore necessary for them to know the ways in which conventions of punctuation differ in American English. I considered merging the discussion of American conventions into the main discussions in Part 2, but decided that to do so would probably distract the majority of readers, who will want advice about British conventions only. Accordingly, I have gathered the discussions of differences in American English into Appendix 3. Note that only the *differences* are discussed there. If usage of a mark is virtually identical in American English and British English, you will find no additional notes on that mark in Appendix 3.

My main criterion for including topics

Discussions of punctuation constantly shade over into discussions of formatting. For example, I am frequently asked whether numbers should be separated from headings or sub-headings with a stop, and whether all main words in a heading should have initial capitals:

3. The Influence of X on Y

or

3 The influence of X on Y

An equally frequent query is whether names and addresses in letters should contain full punctuation or no punctuation:

Mr J. Brown,	OR	Mr J Brown
Training Officer,		Training Officer
Specialised Products PLC,		Specialised Products PLC
29–33, High Street,		29–33 High Street
Someplace,		Someplace
Loamshire,		Loamshire
ABI CD2.		ABI CD 2

These are matters of layout or formatting. They are concerned principally with the aesthetic appearance of the text on the page, not with the signalling of meaning. I am content to see either form. It is more important that each writer should conform consistently to a single standard. Find out what standard has been set in your organisation, or establish a standard for yourself, and keep to it.

However, it is not always easy to draw a dividing line between aspects of punctuation and aspects of formatting. For example, are we

discussing punctuation or formatting when we debate how to set out
items in a numbered list within a paragraph? One possibility is:

1. a small initial letter at the start and a semi-colon at the end
   of each item;
2. ....;
3. ....;
4. and a full stop at the end of the final item.

Another possibility is:

1. A capital letter at the start and a full stop at the end of each
   item.
2. ....
3. ....
4. ....

Yet another possibility is:

1. A capital letter at the start and no mark at all at the end of
   any item
2. ....
3. ....
4. ....

Is this a matter of punctuation or formatting? It may be one or the
other, depending on whether the items in the list are intended to be
genuine completions of the thought in the introductory sentence, or
whether they are simply displayed in list form as a convenient means
of emphasis. This topic is discussed fully on page 28.

Of course, signalling of meaning is not completely separable from
formatting; but in deciding what to include in this book, I have used
this criterion: topics for inclusion must be concerned mainly with
signalling meaning and tone, not just with formatting or neatness.

Not included: punctuation marks as symbols in computing, mathematics, and other scientific work

Part 2 of this book outlines the main conventions of punctuation in English. These conventions will serve you well in general expression of scientific and technical information. However, some punctuation marks (for example, full stop or dot, colon, slash, brackets) are used in special ways as symbols or characters in texts about computing, mathematics, and other scientific topics. Special care is needed in the preparation and printing of such texts, which must conform to national and international standards. I cannot include in this book a summary of the dozens of handbooks, guides, and lists that present the standards for nomenclature and punctuation agreed by professional organisations and by national and international bodies. For guidance on the setting of mathematical and scientific material, I recommend that you refer to a guide from a major publishing house, such as *New Hart's Rules* (Oxford University Press) or *The Chicago Manual of Style* (University of Chicago Press). Additionally, it may be appropriate for you to refer to international standards such as International Standard (ISO) 31/0: 1992 *Specification for quantities, units and symbols*, and *The Units of Measurement Regulations 2001* (*Statutory Instrument 2001 No. 55*) available from the Office of Public Sector Information website, which emphasises the deadline of 31st December 2009 for the end of the authorised use of supplementary indications in conjunction with metric units. Be guided particularly by standards published by your professional association (for example, the *Handbook for Chemical Society Authors*).

Acknowledgement

Like all teachers, I owe an immense amount to the 'students' who have attended my courses. The word 'students' is in inverted commas because I wish to include not only my university audiences, but also the participants in my courses in industry, research centres, and government organisations. This book covers the points that have been raised most frequently by practitioners in computing, engineering, medicine, and science during discussions of their day-to-day problems in reading and writing. Virtually all the example material in the book has come from real documents. When you look at some of the unpunctuated extracts I discuss, you may be tempted to think: 'But surely nobody would write like that'. I am afraid somebody did.

I have been encouraged to write the book because of the exasperation I have heard expressed over the years. With increasing frequency, I have been asked: 'Just what *are* the rules? Nobody ever taught me punctuation in school'. Here is a set of guidelines. I cannot guarantee that, if you follow them, all that you write will become clear instantly to your readers. I *can* say that you will give your readers the best chance of being able to concentrate on the information you want your words to present.

Special thanks

Special thanks to Peter Hunt, who has worked with me in the University of Wales and in industrial courses for more than 30 years, and who has made invaluable contributions to the numerous drafts of this book that we have tried out in our courses.

Special thanks, too, to Jean and Richard Chisholm for their generous help in the preparation of the appendix on conventions of punctuation in the USA.

A request for feedback

In the discussions in this book, I have kept grammatical terminology to a minimum. I have done so because I know that the principal audience I want to address – not language specialists, but practising engineers and scientists – has scant knowledge of that terminology.

In recent years, many teachers of English in schools have ceased to explain the structure of English, and how English works as a code for communication. Through no fault of their own, many young engineers and scientists are now not equipped with the terminology needed for detailed linguistic discussion. Accordingly, I have aimed at making my advice accessible and convincing without resorting to too many grammatical terms. However, I have used *some*. I need to know if I have used too many. If you do not find the advice comprehensible or convincing, or if you find gaps where you needed help, please let me know, so that I can make future editions as useful as possible to everyone who seeks help with punctuation.

From FULL MARKS to PUNCTUATION MATTERS

This book began life as a set of notes entitled *Points on Punctuation* circulated to students in my university courses and industrial training programmes in the 1970s. The first formal edition, entitled *Full Marks: advice on punctuation for scientific and technical writing*, was produced in 1989 in A4 format, printed by the Ashford Press, Southampton, and published and distributed by the Institute of Scientific and Technical Communicators Ltd, London. A second edition followed in 1993, in standard book form, printed by the Ashford Press, and published and distributed by my consultancy, under the business name Ramsbury Books. A third edition, with minor updates, appeared in 1999, again under the imprint of Ramsbury Books, and has been reprinted at least once a year ever since.

I am grateful to Routledge for producing this fourth edition, to be published as a companion volume to my Routledge book *Good Style: writing for science and technology*, with a new title *Punctuation Matters*. This has given me the opportunity to update the references in my text to authorities on punctuation – authorities on British English conventions, such as *New Hart's Rules* and the *New Oxford Dictionary for Writers and Editors* (both themselves updated in 2005), *Copy-Editing: the Cambridge Handbook*, updated (third edition) in 1992, and the Collins Cobuild volumes on *English Grammar* (2005) and *English Usage* (2004); and authorities on American English conventions, such as the *Chicago Manual of Style*, updated (15th edition) in 2003, *Merriam-Webster's Manual for Writers and Editors*, published in 1998 as a revision of *Webster's Standard American Style Manual* (1985), and *Merriam-Webster's Collegiate Dictionary* (11th edition 2003).

However, in the 35 years in which this text has existed in various forms, the conventions of punctuation in English have not changed dramatically. General handling of language, especially in speech, is much influenced by passing fashions of usage and delivery, but conventions of formal writing change only slowly. In this revised edition of my advice, I have pinpointed changes that I believe are significant, and introduced examples to illustrate those changes.

John Kirkman
Ramsbury
Wiltshire

January 2006

Conventions used in this book

Ways of focusing on words and phrases

In this book, I wanted to reserve italic type for giving emphasis to words and phrases in the paragraphs of discussion. That meant I had to find another way of focusing on individual words or phrases taken from my examples. I decided to set up these conventions:

For emphasis on words in
the commentary and discussion: *italic type*

For focusing on words or phrases
taken from examples: <u>underlining</u>

For explaining or defining words
that are the subject of discussion
in the text: 'inverted commas'

Bibliography

Sources of quotations are referred to in the text simply by title, with page numbers in square brackets. Full details of the sources are given in an alphabetical bibliography on pages 138–139.

About the author

John Kirkman was formerly Director of the Communication Studies Unit at the University of Wales Institute of Science and Technology, Cardiff, now Cardiff University, UK. Since 1983, he has worked full-time as a consultant on scientific and technical communication. He has consulted for more than 350 organisations in 23 countries.

He has been a Visiting Lecturer in Technical Communication at the University of Michigan, USA, and at the Massachusetts Institute of Technology, USA, and a Visiting Fellow in Linguistics at Princeton University, USA. He has published more than 70 articles, and has written, edited or contributed to 10 books, including *Effective Writing* (with Christopher Turk, Spon, 1989) and *Good Style: writing for science and technology* (Routledge 2005). The Society for Technical Communication (USA) gave him its Outstanding Article Award in 1974, and an Award for Distinguished Technical Communication (shared with Peter Hunt) in 1987.

Part I

Policy

Stops should be used as sparingly as sense will permit: but in so far as they are needed for an immediate grasp of the sense or for the avoidance of any possible ambiguity, or occasionally to relieve a very lengthy passage, they should be used as freely as need be. The best punctuation is that of which the reader is least conscious; for when punctuation, or the lack of it, obtrudes itself, it is usually because it offends.

G. V. Carey, *Mind the Stop* [p22]

Difficulties caused by lack of punctuation

Time and again, as I read scientific and technical texts, I am obliged to go back and re-read stretches of words. My difficulty is not caused by unfamiliar terms: I have to re-read because writers do not show where units of meaning are supposed to begin and end.

Consider the following extract. I had to read it twice before I was able to interpret it correctly. Do you have to do the same, and if so, why?

> As the machine develops the forms we use to record data from past projects will be amended ...

Most people begin to interpret that sentence as a statement about a machine developing some forms; but then they have to adjust their understanding as they progress further along the lines. No doubt you can see the cause of disturbance. If the writer had provided a comma after the preliminary word-group, you would not have had to stop and re-read the extract:

> As the machine develops, the forms we use to record data from past projects will be amended ...

Here is another extract, which causes difficulty for readers in a different way:

> He draws an analogy between this and the learning process of a new-born child as it develops into maturity and quotes Freud: ...

To read that comfortably (and without a smile at the ambiguity), we need a comma before <u>and quotes Freud</u>:

> He draws an analogy between this and the learning process of a new-born child as it develops into maturity, and quotes Freud: ...

You may be surprised by the suggestion that a comma should be put before <u>and</u>. Teachers of English seem to have left many people with a feeling that it is a cardinal sin to do such a thing. There are some circumstances in which a comma is not needed before <u>and</u>, and some in which it is. That point is discussed fully in Part 2, page 46.

The next example illustrates a third type of difficulty caused when a writer carelessly omits punctuation:

> ... data sheets on equipment below unit level form part of the production documents which are commercially confidential ...

As written, this statement implies that there are some production documents that *are* commercially confidential, and some that are not. We interpret the statement in that way because there is no comma between <u>documents</u> and the word-group <u>which are commercially confidential</u>. Unfortunately, the writer wanted to imply that *all* production documents are commercially confidential. He should have signalled this by inserting a comma after <u>documents</u>:

> ... data sheets on equipment below unit level form part of the production documents, which are commercially confidential ...

This example is important. It shows how relationships between words in a statement are signalled both by the presence and by the *absence* of punctuation marks. We use word-groups beginning with <u>which</u> either to define or to comment, and the precise function is signalled to the reader by the presence or the absence of a comma. That point is discussed fully in Part 2, pages 38 to 42.

For a fourth illustration of how faulty punctuation causes discomfort and ambiguity in technical writing, here is an example of careless omission of hyphens:

> An advantage of Product 85 is that it is easy to use material that has been developed on the basis of experience with Product 84 ...

That sentence seems to make sense: but I discovered from discussions with the writer that he intended to say:

> An advantage of Product 85 is that it is easy-to-use material that has been developed on the basis of experience with Product 84 ...

In revising all these examples, I have not invented revolutionary policies or practices: I have simply introduced signals, punctuation marks, in accordance with established conventions of English. If the writers had used those signals, I should not have had to struggle to make out the meanings they wished to communicate.

The jobs done by punctuation marks

Punctuation marks are integral parts of the signalling system we call writing. They do two jobs. One is *grammatical* and the other is *rhetorical*:

- *grammatical*: they show where the boundaries are meant to be between segments of larger statements, and how segments of text are meant to relate to one another;

- *rhetorical*: they show the emphasis or tone we want to give to a word or word-group.

Here is an example that illustrates the boundary-marking role:

> ... executors delay giving information about substantial devia-tions from agreed dates. Because of this action cannot be taken in time to ...

Did you mis-read that statement at first? The first time I read it, I read Because of this action as a group; but then I realised that the group at the beginning of the second sentence was intended to be just Because of this. If the writer had supplied a comma at the meaning-boundary between this and action, I should not have been misled:

> ... executors delay giving information about substantial devia-tions from agreed dates. Because of this, action cannot be taken in time to ...

Note how punctuation marks signal the relations between segments of text in the following statements:

> Take no action as the camera operates automatically ...
> (The as ... group tells us *when*)

> Take no action, as the camera operates automatically ...
> (The as ... group tells us *why*)

The words in the two statements are exactly the same, but the relations between the words change in accordance with whether a comma is present or absent.

The next three examples illustrate the rhetorical job done by punctuation marks. Note how they signal the emphasis or tone we want to give a word or word-group – information which, if we were speaking, we would express by inflections of voice:

> This is known as 'exact' replacement of ...

> ... and the line <u>must</u> be active at this moment ...

> Do not touch the connectors. Frequently, the lines remain charged AFTER the power has been switched off!

As all these examples show, punctuation marks (including the use of capital letters, underlining, and italics) are vital parts of our signalling system. They are not just optional extras.

Let me emphasise again that it is not just the presence of a punctuation mark that signals something to a reader. In the <u>Take no action ...</u> examples, the *absence* of a comma was as significant as the presence of a comma.

We must not, therefore, include or omit punctuation marks on grounds of appearance. The remark 'Too many stops and commas make the text look spotty' ignores the proper function of punctuation. (Yes, that remark *was* offered in a discussion of effective writing during one of my courses!)

The following text is far from 'spotty': it has no punctuation at all. I present it here to emphasise how much we rely on punctuation signals as we attempt to read a text. Notice that our struggle to comprehend the text is not caused by the difficulty of the ideas: we struggle because we cannot 'see' or 'hear' where statements start or finish. Even some of the smaller word-groups are puzzling until the punctuation signals are supplied. Fortunately, the second version (which is what the author wrote) helps us see at once what is being said:

> the printer has back up files that store reports and statements if the printer should stop working while reports or statements are being printed the information is not lost as it is held on the

printers back up files until it is successfully printed on all back up files five digit numbers are used as identifiers when a new back up file is created a record of it is entered in the daily log once printed information from each back up file is normally purged from the system however the optional save routine enables users to make copies of back up files these can be kept and printed in future in this way the stores in the main system are not unnecessarily filled with saved reports and statements

The printer has back-up files that store reports and statements. If the printer should stop working while reports and statements are being printed, the information is not lost, as it is held on the printer's back-up files until it is successfully printed. On all back-up files, five-digit numbers are used as identifiers. When a new back-up file is created, a record of it is entered in the daily log. Once printed, information from each back-up file is normally purged from the system. However, the optional SAVE routine enables users to make copies of back-up files. These can be kept, and printed in future. In this way, the stores in the main system are not unnecessarily filled with saved reports and statements.

The relation of punctuation to intonation and stress

How do we decide where to put punctuation marks? Roughly, we can say that we use punctuation marks in place of the intonation signals we would use if we were speaking. (This is a generalisation that would not satisfy professional linguists, but it is a convenient starting-point for our discussion.)

As we talk to one another, we 'punctuate', 'emphasise', or 'give colour to' our speech by changing intonation, stress, speed, rhythm, and voice quality. Also, we accompany our words with a wide range of 'body language', such as gestures, shifts of stance, movements of the head and eyes, facial expressions, and other physical movements.

Similarly, if you watch people writing, you will see body language accompanying the *act* of writing. Tongues are stuck out and clenched between teeth; bottom lips are chewed; bodies hunch upwards and forward over the paper as concentration increases; heads tip from side to side; pens move with firmer strokes and increasing speed as points of emphasis are successfully caught in the flow of words to paper;

triumphant arrival at the end of a well-turned sentence is marked by a satisfied thump of the pen to create the full stop; the word-processor ENTER key is struck with an emphatic 'so there' as the final, polished version of a chunk of text is transferred from the screen to a file.

Unfortunately, readers of our texts cannot hear the voice cues we should like them to hear as accompaniment to our words. They cannot see the reinforcing signals we convey by body-language during the act of writing. So we use punctuation marks to signal at least some of the logical and rhetorical information that we pass in speech by means of non-language cues.

There is not a complete list of equivalent signals. For example, there is no punctuation mark that equates to the smile, giggle, or frown that can accompany a group of words. Fortunately, however, when we write about science and technology, we rarely wish to transmit emotional overtones or to 'load' our account. Emotions and opinions often play prominent parts when we discuss commerce, literature, sport, politics, or religion, so we frequently need to use rhetorical signals in writing about those topics; but in most writing about science and technology, our emotions and opinions play a much smaller part, so we need a narrower range of non-linguistic cues. We are able to concentrate mainly on the grammatical and logical functions of punctuation.

So do not despair if your school-teachers gave you little formal guidance about the conventions of punctuation. Almost certainly, you have developed a sense of how to mark the logic and rhetoric of your message in speech. You can use that sense as a starting-point for learning how to punctuate skilfully. As you write, think about the voice cues you would use if you were trying to make clear just what you were saying to an audience. Then translate those cues into written signals.

Look back at the punctuated version of the text on back-up files (page 7). Read it aloud, and notice how your intonation-changes and pauses are reflected by the punctuation marks. Notice, too, that you can move confidently along the lines, never being uncertain whether or not you are grouping words in accordance with the writer's intention. Then read through the unpunctuated text again (pages 6 and 7), and notice how you move in a series of false starts and re-readings, because you are constantly slipping past unmarked boundaries.

Is 'open' or 'light' punctuation enough?

Occasionally, I have been told that 'open' or 'light' punctuation (which frequently seems to mean nothing but full stops) is all that is needed, because readers can see easily the word-groups the writer intended. For example, because hyphens are signals that we use mainly in small word-groups, and because most readers have a span of perception ('eye-span') that can cover two or three words comfortably, hyphens are unnecessary in such small groups.

That argument is seductive, especially because it reduces the effort required from writers. It might be acceptable if, during the process of reading, our eyes always landed conveniently on groups of words that are intended to be linked units. Regrettably, reading does not work like that. Advocates of 'open' punctuation ignore the physical facts about the way we read. Also, they ignore the fact that *absence* of punctuation marks is often as significant as *presence*. Open punctuation frequently obliges readers to read to and fro over texts in order to work out where the meaning-boundaries or changes of tone are supposed to be.

How punctuation helps reading

The physical and mental processes by which we read and comprehend are complex and not fully understood. However, we *do* know that reading is not a simple matter of moving our eyes in a smooth, continuous motion along the lines of text. Our eyes move in a series of jumps, and reading takes place only when the eyes are still. Each time the eye lands on the line, it 'reads' an area of text to each side (and above and below) the landing point. In technical terms, at each 'fixation', we have a certain span of perception or 'eye-span'.

What we can *see* does not seem to vary much from reader to reader. Most of us can span three to five words at each fixation. But what we can *read* is a different matter. It varies in accordance with the effort made by the reader to take in the information at the outer limits of the eye-span. We focus fully on the centre of the fixation; towards the outer limits, we require greater and greater efforts to bring the writing into focus. At each fixation, efficient readers take in more than inefficient readers; efficient readers therefore require fewer fixations to move across a complete line.

However, *all* readers need maximum help to see whether the words they have just read in a fixation make up a complete unit, or whether the meaning will not be complete until they have absorbed words from at least one more fixation. Punctuation marks are major elements – important visual signals – in the help writers can give.

Unfortunately, the word-groups that we see in each fixation do not necessarily make up complete segments of meaning in the sentence we are reading. Sometimes, the centre of a fixation is the white space between words. Sometimes, a comfortable eye-span covers exactly a two- or three-word group. Most frequently, however, it covers either more than one segment of meaning, or only a fragment of a segment.

For example, consider the implications of seeing these words in your first fixation on a line:

Version 1. ... increased. Pressure rises. ...

Version 2. ... increased. Pressure rises ...

Version 3. ... increased. Pressure rises, ...

Version 4. ... increased. Pressure-rises ...

The first word, <u>increased</u>, obviously belongs to the words and meaning you absorbed from your last fixation at the end of the previous line. The full stop after <u>increased</u>, plus one character-space, signals that a new sentence is about to begin. And then you have two more words.

From your past experience of English, you know that the words <u>Pressure rises</u> in Version 1 constitute a complete statement. How do you know that? Because <u>rises</u> is followed by a full stop.

The same words in Version 2 do not express a complete statement. So far, you seem to have just a subject (<u>Pressure</u>) and a verb (<u>rises</u>). Probably, an expression such as 'in proportion to temperature' will follow.

The words <u>Pressure rises</u>, in Version 3 also express an incomplete statement. How do you know? The comma signals that there is more to come. Again, you seem to have a subject and a verb, so far; but the comma also tells you that those two words are to be understood as a complete interim group, and that you can expect something like an enlarging comment or a second part of the statement to follow:

FOR EXAMPLE: Pressure rises, usually only slowly, and ...

OR: Pressure rises, and consequently the outer skin
expands ...

In Version 4, <u>Pressure</u> and <u>rises</u> again constitute an incomplete statement. Indeed, all you have so far is a subject for the next sentence. How do you know? Because the hyphen signals that <u>pressure</u> and <u>rises</u> are to be read as a compound. Probably, a verb such as <u>occur</u> will follow:

... increased. Pressure-rises occur, and ...

These examples illustrate the vital part played by punctuation marks in the process of seeing and understanding what is written on a page. From each fixation, our eyes send our brains visual images – the words and punctuation marks on the page. Then, in our 'minds', or short-term memories, we sort out the meaning. We sort out how the words are intended to relate to one another; we attempt to evaluate the truth and value of what we are reading; we attempt to relate new information to information we possess already; we attempt to decide what to abandon immediately and what to remember – what to pass into long-term memory.

While all this is going on in our minds, our eyes move on to the next fixation, and pass back more visual images. Fortunately, our brains are astoundingly efficient at coping rapidly with the incoming information. But if that information is intrinsically difficult, we have to slow our forward progress because we have to 'think harder' about what is coming in. And if the signals on the page are confusing, our progress is badly hampered: we are not free to concentrate on comprehending the meaning contained in the words; we have first to stop and work out how the encoding on the page has gone awry.

Consider the amount of 'working out' you have to do in this longer example. Imagine that you are reading a technical text, and you begin this sentence:

The high voltage ...

According to the normal conventions of English, when you arrive at a group like that – an adjective (<u>high</u>) followed by a noun (<u>voltage</u>) – with no punctuation signal between them, you can assume that the adjective qualifies the noun: the two words constitute a complete meaning-group. So your mind interprets those first three words as a group. You predict that a statement is beginning about a high voltage, and you move on to find the next recognisable meaning-group.

You register the next word, <u>breakdown</u>:

> The high voltage breakdown ...

You now have to pause to make a quick adjustment. Plainly, the notion you are intended to formulate in your mind is not of a <u>voltage</u> that is high, but of a <u>breakdown</u> at high voltage. You make the adjustment, and move on.

But then you arrive at <u>effects</u>:

> The high voltage breakdown effects ...

Another pause is needed. Is <u>effects</u> a verb? Can you expect the next word to tell you about the changes brought about by the high voltage? You have to look ahead.

You find that the next two words are <u>must be</u>:

> The high voltage breakdown effects must be ...

Ah! The word <u>effects</u> must have been intended as a noun, part of a group 'breakdown effects'. So you have to go back and re-group all the words in the sentence so far:

> The high-voltage breakdown-effects must be taken into account when ...

Of course, your eye and mind work to and fro over the words in a fraction of the time it has taken me to discuss the process of reading and comprehension; but you have to do this work unnecessarily. If the writer had supplied the hyphens, you would have been able to move forward without uncertainty.

Reducing uncertainty by punctuating carefully

Punctuation is principally concerned with the reduction of uncertainty. Can you comprehend immediately the meaning intended in each of the following examples, or are you conscious of momentary hesitations as you reassure yourself about what the writers probably meant?

... lines showing high voltage ratings will be ...
... the tubes suffer from an initial high intensity burst of ...
... the application of a high performance paint ...
... if high pressure readings are obtained from ...
... maintained a steady high recovery efficiency throughout ...
... will be deployed across high speed networks ...
... creates an unusually high speed reduction ...
... the value of the high speed of the ABC line is its ...

The writers of all these extracts were following a policy of 'open' punctuation. I contend that they have abandoned responsibility for giving us maximum help in reducing uncertainty. If conventional punctuation signals had been inserted, we would have been able to see *immediately* the relations between words intended by the writers:

... lines showing high voltage-ratings will be ...
... the tubes suffer from an initial high-intensity burst of ...
... the application of a high-performance paint ...
... if high pressure-readings are obtained from ...
... maintained a steady, high, recovery efficiency throughout ...
... will be deployed across high-speed networks ...
... creates an unusually high speed-reduction ...
... the value of the high speed of the ABC line is its ...

The absence of marks in the final example emphasises the fact that, in signalling meaning, the absence of marks is as important as the presence of marks.

As we set off along lines of print, we do not know what words we shall meet, or how those words will be meant to fit together. We move forward as fast as we can, and we interpret the strings of words in accordance with the norms of English grammatical arrangement and the conventions of English punctuation.

In effect, we rely heavily on guesswork – or to put it more respectably, on prediction. We predict, on the basis of our experience of normal encoding in English, what is likely to come next. If we see The high-pressure ..., we know that another word must be added before the group is complete; so we wait for that word before we construct a segment of meaning in our short-term memories. If we see The high pressure- ..., we know that another element must be added before the group is complete; so we wait for that element before we pass that group into short-term memory. If we see The high pressure ... it looks like a complete unit, so we interpret it that way, and move on. If the writer's signalling is careless or inept, we are misled. We have to look and think back, to adjust our interpretation. The more we have to make adjustments of this type, the greater the sense of struggle we feel as we attempt to grasp the message the words are intended to convey.

When I am reading scientific and technical documents, I have quite enough to do in coping with the difficulty of the ideas being expressed. I resent having to make extra efforts because writers have not signalled clearly the relations they intended between words and word-groups.

I acknowledge readily that few of us would have read the sentence about high-voltage breakdown-effects in the word-by-word way I analysed it. Few of us read only one or two words at a time. Most of us would have covered the words in that example in three or four fixations, beginning with a fixation on or about the first word of the sentence. Nevertheless, the analysis emphasises the way in which the mind's interpreting activity has to be separate from the activity of seeing. It shows why the mind benefits from being given exact signals to indicate how words in separate fixation-groups are intended to go together in segments of meaning.

Absence of punctuation may damage your credibility

Sometimes, absence of punctuation is damaging simply because it suggests to readers that the writer is careless. Without proper punctuation, the words on the page make a weird statement that gives readers a laugh, at the writer's expense. The unpunctuated text may not be incomprehensible, but its apparent carelessness may be damaging to the writer's credibility.

For example, this sign (from London Heathrow Airport) is so ludicrous that, after only a moment's thought, we understand the intended meaning:

NO ELECTRICAL PASSENGER
CARRYING VEHICLES BEYOND THIS POINT

Similarly, these statements are sufficiently nonsensical for every reader to be able to work out what they are supposed to mean:

... to identify the heat generating equipment ...
(the heat-generating equipment)

... to remove bacteria carrying dust particles ...
(bacteria-carrying dust particles)

This next statement did not make me laugh: its carelessness irritated me:

... 1ml of the solution was withdrawn using a pipette cooled in solid CO_2 and injected into the chromatograph ...

The first of the three possible interpretations that follow is nonsense; but is the second version or the third version the correct interpretation?

? 1ml of the solution was withdrawn, using a pipette cooled in solid CO_2 and injected into the chromatograph ...
? 1ml of the solution was withdrawn, using a pipette cooled in solid CO_2, and injected into the chromatograph ...
? 1ml of the solution was withdrawn using a pipette, cooled in solid CO_2, and injected into the chromatograph ...

As we read these careless attempts at communication, our faith in the writers' credibility is disturbed: if the people who wrote (and the people who gave managerial approval to) these extracts are so slipshod about expression, can we be confident about their professional standards in general?

Redundancy as helpful reinforcement

The points I have discussed in the last few pages seem to me strong arguments for full, not 'open' punctuation. Nevertheless, you may often be tempted to assert that your words alone seem adequate to show where you intend a meaning-boundary to be. For example:

Beneath the cover some plates showing slight cracking ...

In reviewing a sentence such as this, you may argue that a comma after cover would be redundant. The first four words Beneath the cover some cannot normally be decoded in any way other than as two groups: Beneath the cover and some. However, I contend that I have to read the fourth word before I know that the first three constitute a completed group; a comma after cover would have allowed my mind to 'close' round that group *before* I went on to read the fourth word, giving me a slight but distinct speeding-up of the comprehension process:

Beneath the cover, some plates showing slight cracking ...

Duplication of signals rarely confuses your readers: omission of signals does. The comma is not undesirable redundancy. It is helpful reinforcement:

Beneath the cover plates showing slight cracking ...
(Beneath the cover, plates showing ...)

It is wise to cultivate the habit of putting punctuation in, not of leaving it out.

Hostile, 'open' punctuators have told me that this advice leads to a plethora of unnecessary punctuation. They have been tempted into the 'pickling in brine' fallacy. As Oliver Wendell Holmes put it: 'Just because I say I like sea bathing, that doesn't mean I want to be pickled in brine'. I want just enough punctuation to make the reader's task as simple as possible, no more, no less.

The lazy writer's evasion of responsibility

In my experience, the omission of punctuation is not often the result of a positive, reasoned policy. All too often, it results from a lazy writer's evasion of responsibility. It is part of the attitude that answers all criticism of less-than-precise writing with the shrugging response 'They'll know what it means'. That attitude puts increasing responsibility on readers for working out what a text is intended to mean.

Consider this expression, from a report about noise affecting some new houses:

... is keeping a catalogue of resident complaints ...

The meaning could be:

... complaints that are resident
... complaints from a resident
... complaints from residents
... complaints about a resident
... complaints about residents

The first time I read that expression, I enjoyed the notion of complaints being resident. However, though my concentration on the argument of the whole text was momentarily disturbed, I dismissed rapidly the absurdity of complaints being resident, and assumed I should interpret the expression in one of the other ways. On reflection, I thought the most likely interpretation was 'complaints from residents', though the context did not make clear whether the complaints were from several residents or just one.

The writer told me subsequently that my guess was correct. He argued that it was 'pretty obvious what it meant', and added that typical professional readers (acoustics engineers) would have no difficulty in guessing his intended meaning.

That line of argument depresses me. The writer was prepared to accept imprecision and vagueness that he would certainly not have tolerated in mathematical or engineering activities. Why settle for less precision in writing, especially when the simple provision of an s and an apostrophe (a catalogue of residents' complaints) would have removed all need for guessing?

Here is another expression that gave me trouble:

... for use in a customer network ...

In this example, we have a noun (<u>customer</u>) used to modify another noun (<u>network</u>). In decoding a text in English, our first expectation is that a pre-modifying noun (such as <u>customer</u>) creates a meaning equivalent to a post-modifying <u>of ...</u> construction: for example, <u>waste disposal</u> is equivalent to 'disposal of waste'; <u>grass cutting</u> is equivalent to 'cutting of grass'. So, making my best guess in accordance with probabilities, I interpreted the statement to mean 'for use in a network of customers'.

The text that followed did not seem to make sense if I used that interpretation. Fortunately, I was able to ask the writer what he meant. He meant 'for use in a customer's network'. The omission of the apostrophe and the <u>s</u> led me to a totally wrong interpretation. Was the writer entitled to argue that the punctuation marks were unnecessary, because 'They'll know what it means'?

I accept the argument that, when words suggest two or more meanings, it is reasonable to expect readers to choose the *probable* meaning, not the *im*probable one. But that argument is acceptable only to defend use of a word or phrase that takes on a different meaning in accordance with its context. For example, we could not reasonably complain about the use of <u>pitch</u> in a text about ultrasonics, on the grounds that it *could* be interpreted to refer to the way a ship moves in a rough sea. But the argument is not acceptable as a defence of writing that gives us *unnecessary* interpretative work to do. If there is a conventional signal that makes it unnecessary for readers to examine two or more probable meanings, that conventional signal should be used. The onus for reducing uncertainty lies on the writer, not on the reader.

The best writing is that which enables readers to move forward rapidly and confidently, with the minimum of hesitations and regressions to check what is being said. If we are to write well, we must learn to signal our meaning with maximum clarity: we must learn to handle the conventions of punctuation as carefully as we handle intonation and stress in spoken English.

Part 2

Guidelines

Punctuation too often ranks as an adjunct. In the fact, it should rank as a component. It is not something that one applies as an ornament, for it is part of the structure; so much a part that, without it, the structure would be meaningless – except after an exhausting examination.

Eric Partridge, *You Have a Point There* [p8]

The work of punctuation is to show, or hint at, the grammatical relation between words, phrases, clauses, and sentences; but it must not be forgotten that stops also serve to regulate pace, to throw emphasis on particular words and give them significance, and to indicate tone. ... Secondly, it is a sound principle that as few stops should be used as will do the work. ... Thirdly, ... they are to be regarded as devices, not for saving the writer the trouble of putting his words into the order that naturally gives the required meaning, but for saving his reader the moment or two that would sometimes, without them, be necessarily spent on reading the sentence twice over ...; stops are not to alter meaning, but merely to show it up.

H. W. and E. G. Fowler, *The King's English* [p233–234]

Apostrophe (')

1.1 Indicating possessives

Use an apostrophe to indicate the possessive form of nouns:

The group's proposals were discussed at length ... (singular group)

The groups' proposals were discussed at length ... (plural groups)

Always use an apostrophe and an *s* to mark a possessive. Beware of the ambiguity created by the omission of both:

... then links up with customer terminating equipment ...
(the customer's terminating equipment)

If the noun you wish to make a possessive already ends with an s̲, you have the option of adding just an apostrophe, or an apostrophe and an s̲:

EITHER ... to one of the chassis' galvanised upper arms ...
OR ... to one of the chassis's galvanised upper arms ...

But preferably re-write the statement to remove the awkward grouping of letters:

... to one of the galvanised upper arms of the chassis ...

Just a reminder: i̲t̲s̲ is the possessive form of i̲t̲. No apostrophe is needed. I̲t̲'s̲ is a contracted form of i̲t̲ i̲s̲. See section 1.4 for advice against using contractions.

1.2 Indicating association or affiliation

It is not necessary to put an apostrophe in phrases such as The Oesophageal Patients Association, the Consulting Engineers Network, The Radio Operators Society, The Boiler Manufacturers Group, the Campaigns Director, a sports reporter, or a clinicians meeting. In these examples, the plural nouns do not indicate possession: they indicate membership of a group or category, or a distinguishing attribute.

1.3 Forming plurals

Usually, form plurals of letters, numbers, symbols, acronyms, or words you are discussing as entities, by simply adding a small s:

> ... found more difficulty with the single A than with the four Bs ...
> ... failed to recognise that 2665 contained two 6s ...
> ... the number of &s in the group ...
> ... is connected to three VDUs and one printer ...
> ... had omitted all the ENTERs from the text ...

It is especially important to distinguish clearly whether acronyms are plurals, possessives, or both:

> ... are connected to the CPUs that have a ... (simple plural)
> ... are connected to the CPU's processors by ... (singular possessive)
> ... are connected to the CPUs' processors by ... (plural possessive)

Occasionally, however, you may want to make a plural of a lower-case letter or symbol. It would be confusing to write:

> ... enter two +s ...
> ... followed by two ys ...
> ... represent decreasing pHs of absorption for these items ...

You could reduce the probability of confusion by inserting apostrophes:

> ... enter two +'s ...
> ... followed by two y's ...
> ... represent decreasing pH's of absorption for these items ...

But the presence of apostrophes might also be confusing, so the best policy is always to try to reconstruct the sentence to avoid difficulty:

... enter + twice ...

... followed by y twice ...

... represent a decreasing pH of absorption for each of these items ...

1.4 Signalling contractions

Apostrophes are correctly used to form contractions like <u>don't</u>, <u>can't</u>, <u>what's</u>, and <u>it's</u>. However, though the advent of 'user-friendly' documentation has encouraged experiments with contractions, many readers still feel that contractions slip below the level of propriety suitable for formal writing in business, industry, and research. So, I recommend that you use contractions only in informal writing, such as hand-written internal memoranda or e-mails to friends and colleagues.

Sometimes an apostrophe is used to indicate that letters have been omitted from an abbreviated word in a column heading or other cramped space. Unfortunately, there are no general rules about which letters you should omit, or about whether you should form abbreviations by contraction or truncation (that is, whether <u>resolution rate</u> should be abbreviated by omitting letters, to give <u>resol'n rate</u>, or by cutting off the end of the word, to give <u>resol. rate</u>). A sensible principle is to omit the smallest number of letters that space will permit, leaving recognisable syllables wherever possible:

    WRITE precip'n rate (precipitation rate)
       OR precip. rate
      NOT pre'tion rate

My main advice, however, is that you or your organisation should establish a usual way of forming abbreviations, and use it consistently.

Capital Letters

2.1 Beginning a sentence

Use a capital letter, sometimes called an upper-case letter, at the beginning of the first word to signal the beginning of a sentence. ('Upper case' and 'lower case' are historical terms derived from two boxes used by printers to hold the type used in old-fashioned type-setting. One box, which held capital letters, was placed above the other, which held small letters.)

2.2 Signalling proper nouns or adjectives

Use initial capitals (capitals for the initial letters of words, but not throughout the words) to signal proper nouns or adjectives, and words derived from proper nouns (a 'proper' noun is the name of a specific person, a place, a country, a month, a day, a holiday, a journal title):

> ... the *volt* is named after Count Alessandro Volta ...
> ... the Darwinian theory of evolution ...
> ... discovered in Boston in January 1864 ...
> ... manufactured in France ...
> ... the French optometrist ...
> ... use the normal English keyboard ...
> ... not be ready before Christmas ...
> ... was published in *Scientific American* in ...

Use a capital for the initial letter of a trade name:

> ... a Plexiglas shield ...
> ... a Rolls Royce engine ...
> ... a Pulsometer pump ...

Use capitals throughout (sometimes described as 'all upper-case') for acronyms or for words used as commands in computing documents:

> ... belong to NATO and therefore ...
> ... written in FORTRAN ...
> ... use the SAVE command to ...

If you wish to use the plural form of an acronym, add an s̲ in lower case:

> WRITE   CPUs
>   NOT   CPUS or CPU's

See also section 1.3 for a discussion of apostrophes in plurals.

Reserve the use of capital letters for proper nouns (names) or specific titles of persons or entities. Avoid the temptation to use capitals when you are using a term in a general way:

> WRITE ... send the results to Pathology Department ...
>   OR ... is a current cause of concern in pathology departments throughout the UK ...
> BUT NOT ... is a current cause of concern in Pathology Departments throughout the UK ...

> WRITE ... the smoothing algorithm uses four waveform samples ...
> BUT NOT ... the Smoothing Algorithm uses four waveform samples ...

Do NOT use capitals for the initial letter of points of the compass, unless they are integral parts of geographical names:

> WRITE ... in the south of England.
>   ... located to the east of the existing warehouse.
>   BUT ... survey of the North Yorkshire region.
>   ... distributed in South Humberside.

Do NOT use capitals for the initial letter of the names of seasons:

> WRITE ... at or about the winter solstice.
>   ... are greater in the autumn (USA: in the fall).

2.3 Capital letters in titles, headings, and sub-headings

The use of capitals in titles, headings, and sub-headings is a matter of choice. The main titles of books and chapters conventionally have had initial capitals for all 'main' words:

A book title: *A Student's Grammar of the English Language*
A chapter heading: *Procedures and Computations in the Analysis of Experiments*

However, modern practice in publishing houses in the UK and the USA varies greatly. Some publishers retain the use of initial capitals for all main words in a book title, but use an initial capital for only the first word of a chapter heading:

Main title: *Designing and Writing Online Documentation*
Chapter heading: *Organizing online documents*

Other publishers use an initial capital for only the first word of a book title:

Design for desktop publishing

Sometimes, variations in capitalisation are used to reinforce the effect of varying font size in headings:

Main chapter heading: *WHOLE HEADING IN CAPITALS*
First level section heading: *Initial Capitals for All Main Words*
Second level section heading: *Initial capital for the first word only*

Since such wide variation is acceptable, the most important point is that you or your organisation should establish a usual way of capitalising titles and headings, and use it consistently.

3

Colon (:)

3.1 'Invoicing': indicating that a list of items will follow

Use a colon to indicate that material is to follow. The material that follows may be a summary, a list, a complete sentence, a question, or a quotation.

If the items in the material that follows the colon consist of only one or two words, they may be separated simply with commas:

> There are many disturbing factors: fatigue, poor eye-sight, poor reading ability, anxiety or undue caution, distractibility, and inadequate motivation.

If each of the items in the following material consists of several words, you will probably be wise to separate them with semi-colons:

> ... in percentiles: scores at the 90th percentile or above are referred to as SG (Selection Grade) 1; 90th to 70th as SG2; 70th to 50th as 3+; 50th to 30th as 3-; 30th to 10th as 4; and scores by the bottom 10 per cent as SG5.

Theoretically, all the material that follows the colon is 'suspended' from it as the completion of the introductory words. When there is only a small amount of material, it can be presented conveniently within your normal paragraph layout:

> ... components required: motor brushes, bearings, and wiring; oil-filled capacitors; tags; cable connectors, lacing and sleeving.

But often you will want to help your reader see the elements in your list, and you will use 'display' tactics to do so – you will inset the list vertically. Again theoretically, you should retain the same pattern of punctuation, with intermediate semi-colons, and a final full stop:

... the principal additions to the keyboard are:

- a transmission key;
- five cursor-control keys;
- an Operator's Guide.

... the specialist in quality assurance must:

- participate in software-planning sessions;
- review and audit software documentation;
- be involved in production of an internal memorandum that specifies quality requirements.

Punctuating displayed text after a colon

However, punctuating displayed text is not as straightforward as I have suggested. There are two complicating factors:

- when we use display technique to help with the completion of a statement, we are tempted to 'hang' overwhelming amounts of information after the colon;

- in technical writing, we use an invoicing colon not only to indicate continuation/completion/extension of a statement but also simply to signal that a special display of information is about to appear.

Think carefully as you plan to hang a list after a colon. Do you genuinely want readers to absorb all the listed information as the completion of a thought begun before the colon? If you do, continuation of your thought is probably best signalled by use of a lower-case letter at the start of each item, a semi-colon at the end of each intermediate item, and a full stop at the end of the complete statement:

Accordingly, baths containing stronger concentrations of zinc are preferred when:

- maximum production rates are demanded;
- wide fluctuations in operating conditions must be tolerated;
- bath contamination is a serious problem.

But consider how much you are asking your readers to absorb in a connected sequence. Almost certainly, if you are tempted to begin new sentences within intermediate items, you will create a pattern of information that is too complex for your readers to absorb easily. You will probably be wise to reconstruct your statement.

For example, this presentation of information about two types of sound is difficult to digest as a continuous statement, because each of the two explanations is itself complex:

When a source of sound is operating in a room or other enclosure, the sound pressure in the room consists of two components:

- direct sound, which is the sound that reaches a point without reflection. Because of divergence, this sound decreases as distance from the source increases. A doubling of distance from the source reduces the sound pressure level by six decibels;
- reverberant sound, which reaches a point after one or more reflections. Approximately, reverberant sound does not depend on the position of the source in the room. It is directly proportional to the total power of the source and inversely proportional to the acoustic absorption of the surfaces in the room.

A small reconstruction makes the message more manageable:

When a source of sound is operating in a room or other enclosure, the sound pressure in the room consists of two components: direct sound and reverberant sound.

Direct sound is the sound that reaches a point without reflection. Because of divergence, this sound decreases as distance from the source increases. A doubling of distance from the source reduces the sound pressure level by six decibels.

Reverberant sound reaches a point after one or more reflections. Approximately, reverberant sound does not depend on the position of the source in the room. It is directly proportional to the total power of the source, and inversely proportional to the acoustic absorption of the surfaces in the room.

The second complicating factor is that, in technical writing, an invoicing colon does not always tell readers to use the material after the colon to complete a thought begun before the colon. In the next example, the colon is simply a signal that display layout is going to be used to emphasise a catalogue of features. The colon is preceded by a complete sentence. Each feature is then stated as a complete sentence (though It is omitted). The list layout is an information-design device, or a device of formatting. In such circumstances, it seems reasonable to use different punctuation – to begin each item with a capital letter, and to end it with a full stop:

The X99 has the following features:

- Fulfils ISO 7726, ANSI/ASHRAE 55–81.

- Measures in SI and imperial units.

- Can store measurements made over a 120-hour period, and re-display them later.

- Has digital parallel and serial interfaces.

- Includes a plug-in battery-pack.

Sometimes, even the full stops are omitted; the writer relies on the layout to make clear the completeness of the items:

Many chemical products can be made from aniline:

- Isocyanates for the urethane industry

- Antioxidants, activators, accelerators and other materials for the rubber industry

- Azo, nigrosine and other dyes and pigments for a variety of applications

- Hydroquinone for the photographic industry

In a similar way, list layout is sometimes used principally to display the existence of several possibilities, with no true sense of 'completion' of a thought before the colon. Each possibility is expressed as a self-contained statement, sometimes consisting of several sentences. It seems reasonable, again, to use a different convention of punctuation in these circumstances – to begin each item with a capital letter, and end with a full stop, as in the following example:

Output is forwarded to any one of these stations, in one of three ways:

- If the ABC user logs on to ABC with the "$station-name" parameter specified, output reports are sent to the station so specified. That station name must be present in the station list of that project, to allow the user to log on.

- If the user logs on without specifying the "$station-name" parameter, output goes to the first station in the project's station list.

- If the user uses a JCL statement that allows him to specify a destination station through the DEST parameter, output goes to that station. JCL statements that permit this include:

  – OUTVAL ... DEST = station-name
  – SYSOUT ... DEST = station-name
  – WRITER ... DEST = station-name

It is often difficult to decide whether a 'colon plus list' layout is being used genuinely to help with the completion of a thought or simply to emphasise a pattern of information. One way to decide is to look at the introductory element before the colon. If the introductory element is an incomplete sentence, punctuate the list with lower-case initial letters, intermediate semi-colons, and a final stop. In this way, you signal to your readers that you want them to connect the listed items closely with the incomplete sentence before the colon. If the introductory element is a complete sentence, punctuate each item in the list with an initial capital letter and a final full stop (or no stop). In this way, you emphasise the comparative independence of the items.

Many organisations now specify that writers use just one method of punctuating all lists in their writing. It seems a pity to lose the ability to signal different functions of the list layout after a colon; but it is certainly wise to ask all writers in a given context to conform to the same convention(s).

Showing sequence or hierarchy in a list after a colon

If you wish to show that the items in your list are in a sequence or hierarchy, use numbers:

    1. .... ;
    2. .... ;
    3. ....

or letters:

    a) .... ;
    b) .... ;
    c) ....

If you wish to show that the items in your list are separate and parallel, but in no significant order or hierarchy, use 'bullets':

    • .... ;
    • .... ;
    • ....

or (sparingly, now that bullets are usually available on word-processing equipment) use dashes:

    – .... ;
    – .... ;
    – ....

Using a colon to precede a direct quotation

If you wish to throw particular emphasis on the formality or weight of a direct quotation, precede it with a colon:

> The researchers concluded: "Most patients with non Q wave myocardial infarction do not benefit from routine early invasive management consisting of coronary angiography and revascularisation."

For a discussion of the various ways of setting out quotations, see pages 78–81.

3.2 Signalling division of a sentence

Use a colon as a stop within a sentence, to show that 'enlarging' information is to follow.

The colon, when used within a sentence, is a 'lighter' stop than a full stop, and joins two statements that are grammatically independent but logically closely related. Usually, the material after the colon is supplementary or amplifying, or sets up an antithesis. Often, the material preceding the colon is general: the material following it is particular or reinforcing. Begin the clause following the colon with a lower-case letter, not a capital letter:

Take care when using this solvent: it may dissolve certain synthetic materials ...

... interaction produces only carbon dioxide: no methanol is formed.

X files are used with the System I package: Y files are used with the System IA package ...

... should not show poor texts during the teaching of technical writing. We have long since abandoned the view that the teaching of morals involves keeping the pupil in ignorance of wickedness: indeed, the appreciation of the good would be meaningless without an equal appreciation of the bad.

4

Comma (,)

4.1 Marking the boundary of a 'preliminary' group

Use a comma to mark the boundary of a 'preliminary' unit at the start of a sentence.

Frequently, we begin sentences with a single word or a longer word-group to indicate time, place, manner, reason, or other information relevant to the main statement that is to follow:

> Tomorrow, ...
> Immediately, ...
> Before reacting, ...
> Without a pause, ...
> In order to increase the output, ...
> If the reaction is too violent, ...

When we are speaking, we help our listeners by signalling the boundary of such preliminary units with a change in intonation and a pause. (Try reading that sentence – and this sentence – aloud. You will hear the changes of tone and timing.) When you are writing, give your readers similar help by signalling the boundaries of preliminary units with commas.

Omission of commas in preliminary positions is one of the commonest causes of confusion for readers. Note how, in reading the following example, you first take in an idea about an <u>assembly load</u>; but then the remainder of the sentence makes plain that you have mis-read the beginning – that the boundary of the first meaning-group is intended to be after <u>assembly</u>:

> To get a clean assembly load the assembled equals table before
> the assembly is run ...

A comma removes the uncertainty:

> To get a clean assembly, load the assembled equals table before
> the assembly is run ...

Occasionally, you may feel that the wording of the sentence leaves
no possibility of the meaning-boundary being missed. Nevertheless,
put the comma in. Train yourself to supply preliminary commas automatically. That way, you will minimise the number of occasions on
which what seemed obvious to *you* is not at all clear to your readers.

If you provide a comma automatically, you will not cause confusion:
you will reinforce your readers' grasp of what you are saying. In contrast, if you make a habit of omitting commas, you will often force
your readers to re-read what you have written. In all of the following
examples, the writer intended what is written in the first version, but
wrote what is in the second – to the great confusion of readers!

MEANT	Frequently, adjusted totals need to be scrutinised ...
WROTE	Frequently adjusted totals need to be scrutinised ...

MEANT	Further, automatic updating of directories should be possible when an ABC workstation is moved from one XYZ address to another ...
WROTE	Further automatic updating of directories should be possible when an ABC workstation is moved from one XYZ address to another ...

MEANT	At present, rates of return giving a net profit of only 7% are widespread in the industry ...
WROTE	At present rates of return giving a net profit of only 7% are widespread in the industry ...

MEANT	Unfortunately though, incorrect predictions were made about both negative and positive experiments, ...
WROTE	Unfortunately though incorrect predictions were made about both negative and positive experiments ...

> MEANT   Should any burner fail to ignite, its respective section
>   will revert to 'purge', and in this way ...
> WROTE   Should any burner fail to ignite its respective section
>   will revert to 'purge' and in this way ...
>
> MEANT   In the event of failure of any of these components to
>   operate, the respective motor will not start until the
>   fault has been rectified ...
> WROTE   In the event of failure of any of these components to
>   operate the respective motor will not start until the
>   fault has been rectified ...

It is particularly important to consider whether or not a comma is needed after <u>However</u> at the beginning of a sentence. A comma after <u>However</u> indicates that we are to take that word to mean 'In contrast with' or 'In spite of' what has just been said:

> However, common practice is to remove the ...

The absence of a comma after However signals that we are to take that word to mean 'no matter how' or 'irrespective of how':

> However common it may be to ignore this input, we should nevertheless ...

In each of the following pairs of examples, the writer wrote the first, but meant the second:

> ... is balanced by the rate of neutralisation. However oxidative stress occurs when the balance is disturbed, through an increase in ...

> ... is balanced by the rate of neutralisation. However, oxidative stress occurs when the balance is disturbed, through an increase in ...

> ... in a multiple sequence alignment (MSA). However important residues may also mutate, with compensatory mutations occurring elsewhere in ...

> ... in a multiple sequence alignment (MSA). However, important residues may also mutate, with compensatory mutations occurring elsewhere in ...

I have been told that I am unduly fussy if I complain about omission of a comma from a sentence that starts:

> However common practice is to remove the ...

After all, the argument goes, a reader has to read only to the fourth word before it is entirely clear what meaning is intended, and can make a rapid mental adjustment.

My reply is that I resent having to read to the fourth word before the meaning of the first becomes plain: careful punctuation could have given me accurate meaning after just one word. In examples such as the following, I had to read a long way into the sentences before I realised that I had been misled:

> However the interpolation board uses its smoothing algorithm to interpolate four successive waveform samples and it does this separately for each of the channels ...

> (adjustment needed when I reached the 15th word <u>and it does this ...</u>)

> ... a mild-steel plate. However the plate is fitted to the pre-stressed concrete beam which supports the left-hand end of the silo, so it cannot ...

> (adjustment needed when I reached the 19th word <u>so it cannot, ...</u>)

> However the disparity between theoretical paint solids content and determined solids ranged between 5 and 6% and was not related to vacuum stripping ...

> (adjustment needed when I reached the 17th word <u>and was not ...</u>)

4.2 Enclosing parenthetic information

Use commas to enclose parenthetic words, phrases, and clauses (parenthetic information is explanatory or qualifying information inserted within a sentence as an extra comment).

In English, we use three sets of marks to enclose parenthetic comments – pairs of commas, pairs of brackets (parentheses), and pairs of dashes. Use commas to mark relatively light grammatical parentheses:

The building, as I have said, will be hexagonal.

The fuel valve, a solenoid gate valve, consists of ...

Use brackets to mark heavy, explanatory additional remarks within statements:

This action is optional (though recommended) and can be ...
We shall need heating (for the average temperature is 34°F) throughout the year.

... gave high readings with the standard dose (though not with 90% of the standard) and it was necessary to ...

Use dashes to create the effect of a deliberate 'aside' within a statement:

The raw data produced by these routines – and there are 17 of them – must be processed within ...

... animals are maintained under hygienic conditions – much more hygienic than prevail in most farms – until their weight ...

... client claims that most of the computing is interactive – though we would not accept this definition – and he therefore needs ...

4.3 Signalling the function of relative clauses

Signal clearly whether you intend a clause that begins with a relative pronoun to *comment* or to *define*.

A relative clause is a clause that begins with <u>who</u>, <u>whose</u>, <u>whom</u>, <u>which</u>, or <u>that</u>:

... discusses only the software *that* you will instal ...
... passes first to the system administrator, *who* decides whether or not to allow the entry, and then on to ...
... is accepted by the operator *whose* load is the lightest ...
... the manager from *whom* the request has been received ...
... the sand grains, *which* are almost entirely quartz, are not cemented together ...

Roughly speaking, we use relative clauses either to *define* an element in an earlier part of the statement or to *comment* on an earlier part of the statement. (The usual grammatical terms, which you may find helpful, are that a defining group is 'restrictive', and that a commenting group is 'non-restrictive'. If you would like a detailed account of the use of relative clauses, I recommend *Collins Cobuild English Grammar*, p362–70.)

The presence or absence of a comma before a relative pronoun is very important in signalling to your reader the meaning you intend. Here are examples of defining use and commenting use:

A six-month-old calf was submitted for examination, showing lameness in all four legs which had been present since soon after birth.
(The <u>which ...</u> clause *defines*: it relates to *legs*, and tells us that the legs had been present since soon after birth)

A six-month-old calf was submitted for examination, showing lameness in all four legs, which had been present since soon after birth.
(The <u>which ...</u> clause *comments*: it relates to *lameness*, and tells us that the lameness had been present since soon after birth)

Unfortunately, the writer wrote the first, nonsensical, statement, but meant the second! The first of the following statements would produce much more expensive activity than the second (which is what the writer intended):

Replace the fuel lines and electrical conduits, which have cracks or damaged B-nut fittings ...
(the <u>which ...</u> clause comments, is non-restrictive: it implies that *all* the fuel lines and electrical conduits are faulty)

Replace the fuel lines and electrical conduits which have cracks or damaged B-nut fittings ...
(the <u>which ...</u> clause defines, is restrictive: it implies that only faulty fuel lines and electrical conduits are to be replaced)

A writer wrote in a discussion paper:

> Planning authorities should provide alternative locations for small businesses, which are or would be offensive in a residential area ...

He did not intend to comment that *all* small businesses are offensive in a residential area: he wanted to restrict his remark just to the types of businesses that would be offensive. He should have written:

> Planning authorities should provide alternative locations for small businesses which are or would be offensive in a residential area ...

In deciding whether or not to put a comma before your <u>which ...</u> group, you may find the following mnemonic useful:

<u>C</u>ommenting clauses need a <u>c</u>omma,
<u>d</u>efining clauses <u>d</u>on't.

See how it applies to the following pairs of examples:

> ... the <u>n</u> data bits are then transmitted to the receiving machine which performs the arithmetic on the <u>n</u> bits ...
> (restrictive, or defining: implies that there are several receiving machines, and points to the one that performs the arithmetic)

> ... the <u>n</u> data bits are then transmitted to the receiving machine, which performs the arithmetic on the <u>n</u> bits ...
> (non-restrictive, or commenting: implies that there is only one receiving machine, and comments that the arithmetic is performed by that machine)

> The power loss can be reduced by switching the transmitter direct to the X aerial which is mounted on the roof ...
> (restrictive, or defining: explains which of several X aerials is being referred to)

> The power loss can be reduced by switching the transmitter direct to the X aerial, which is mounted on the roof ...
> (non-restrictive, or commenting: explains where the single X aerial is sited)

... headings which contain up to 64 characters must not include
...
(restrictive or defining)

... headings, which contain up to 64 characters, must not include
...
(non-restrictive or commenting)

... operates by creating a glow discharge in the source chamber
which contains argon at half-torr pressure ...
(restrictive, or defining)

... operates by creating a glow discharge in the source chamber,
which contains argon at half-torr pressure ...
(non-restrictive, or commenting)

English teachers may have told you previously that you should
always signal restrictive intention by starting your relative clause with
that. Indeed, it is a good general habit to adopt:

The law that was introduced to uphold the freedom of indus-
trialists to ...

We shall re-build the wall that is dangerous before we consider
...

... must renegotiate the off-shore lease that falls due in two
months from now ...

But in acceptable modern English usage, that and which are often
interchanged. For example, all the italicised clauses in the following
sentences were intended to be restrictive (defining) clauses, but some
are introduced by that and some by which:

The balance potentiometers permit the cancellation of any drift
that may exist in the servo controls ...

The Lagrange method is one *that does not require the independent
variable to be equi-spaced* ...

In the experiment *which lasted two hours,* ...

The pitch control is a multiple switch *which controls the pitch
datum motor* ...

A tab washer is a sheet-metal detail *that is placed below a nut or screw-head* ...

Also, in clauses that begin with <u>in which,</u> <u>by which,</u> or <u>through which,</u> it is not possible to convert <u>which</u> to <u>that</u> as an indication of a defining clause:

... the orifice, through which the exhaust gases leave the chamber, is larger than ...
(commenting)

... the orifice through which the exhaust gases leave the chamber is larger than ...
(defining)

... there is no method by which the piles can be inspected other than excavation ...
(defining)

... evaluate results of the trial in which elemental iron particles up to 3.0 mm in size were permitted ...
(defining)

So the accurate use of commas is vital. Remember the mnemonic: <u>c</u>ommenting clauses need a <u>c</u>omma; <u>d</u>efining clauses <u>d</u>on't.

4.4 Indicating the function of <u>with ...</u> constructions and <u>-ing...</u> constructions

A similar important use of commas is to indicate which earlier part of a sentence a <u>with ...</u> construction or an <u>-ing ...</u> construction is intended to refer back to; usually (but not always), the presence or absence of a comma tells us whether the <u>with ...</u> construction or <u>-ing ...</u> construction is intended to be adjectival or adverbial:

Insert the new disk into the disk drive with the notch at the bottom ...
(adjectival: the <u>with ...</u> construction refers to the *disk drive*)

Insert the new disk into the disk drive, with the notch at the bottom ...
(adverbial: the <u>with ...</u> construction tells us how to *insert* the new disk)

Return the XYZ to the operator following the ABC routine ...
(adjectival: the <u>following ...</u> construction refers to the *operator*)

Return the XYZ to the operator, following the ABC routine ...
(adverbial: the <u>following ...</u> construction tells us when to *return* the XYZ)

X is an effective acute, oral treatment for migraine with a rapid onset of action
(adjectival: the <u>with ...</u> construction refers to the *migraine*)

X is an effective acute, oral treatment for migraine, with a rapid onset of action
(adjectival: the <u>with ...</u> construction tells us that the *treatment* has a rapid onset of action)

These glycans are poorly transferred to proteins resulting in unoccupied glycolisation sequons.
(adjectival: the <u>resulting ...</u> construction refers to the *proteins*)

These glycans are poorly transferred to proteins, resulting in unoccupied glycolisation sequons.
(adverbial: the <u>resulting ...</u> construction tells us the result of the *poor transfer*)

Reject the applicant using procedure XYZ ...
(adjectival: the <u>using ...</u> construction refers to the *applicant*)

Reject the applicant, using procedure XYZ ...
(adverbial: the <u>using ...</u> construction tells us how to *reject* the applicant)

The relative reinforcing effects of nicotine were assessed after the end of generalisation testing using a choice procedure.
(adjectival: the <u>using ...</u> construction refers to the *testing*)

The relative reinforcing effects of nicotine were assessed after the end of generalisation testing using a choice procedure.
(adverbial: the <u>using ...</u> construction tells us how the effects were *assessed*)

In particular, check carefully every time you write a <u>using ...</u> construction: careless punctuation often creates nonsensical statements:

> ... in a recent study in which clinical signs indicative of PMWS
> were reproduced in a pig using an isolate of PCV-2 from a herd
> in Sweden.

> ... management of advanced tracheal collapse in dogs using intra-
> luminal self-expanding biliary wallstents.

Your readers may smile at such statements, but their concentration
on the argument of your text will have been disturbed.

4.5   Separating adjectives in a series

Use commas to separate two or more adjectives in a series, when you
want each separately to qualify the final noun.

We use commas in this way to save using several <u>and</u>s. To describe
a <u>response</u> as early, and quantifiable, and hyperplastic, we could write:

> ... an early and quantifiable and hyperplastic response ...

But by convention, we substitute commas for the <u>and</u>s:

> ... an early, quantifiable, hyperplastic response ...

In this way, we emphasise that each adjective separately qualifies the
noun <u>response</u>: we show that <u>quantifiable</u> is not meant to qualify
<u>hyperplastic</u>, a mis-reading that readers might make if there were no
commas or <u>and</u>s:

> ... an early quantifiable hyperplastic response ...

Use commas, then, in sequences such as:

> ... single, variable inputs ...
> ... an unmanned, high-capacity, offshore well ...
> ... an extensive, twin-site, development plan ...
> ... a light, adjustable frame ...
> ... a mobile, air-operated starter ...
> ... splitpins have an anti-corrosive, thin-layer, gold finish ...

However, it is not usual to put a comma between a numeral and another adjective:

WRITE ... three plastic-coated cables ...
NOT ... three, plastic-coated cables ...

and it is not usual to put a comma after an adjective that qualifies the adjective that follows:

WRITE ... a bright red label ...
NOT ... a bright, red label ...

But you may need to reconstruct your sentence, or to supply a hyphen, if ambiguity could arise:

WRITE ... the skirt can be moved away from the groove if changes are made to two dimensions, one to the width of the skirt, and one to the width of the dome ...
NOT ... the skirt can be moved away from the groove if two dimensional changes are made, one to the width of the skirt, and one to the width of the dome ...

WRITE ... a light-green box ...
NOT ... a light green box ...

WRITE ... using airborne-noise criteria from ...
NOT ... using airborne noise criteria from ...

See also the discussion of linking words with hyphens to form compounds in section 9.1.

4.6 Separating two word-groups referring to a single following word

When two or more words or word-groups refer to a single following word, use commas to separate the words or word-groups from each other and from the following word:

This is a popular, though time-consuming, technique.
... go through an iterative, but not unduly repetitive, procedure.
... gives a clear, though very small, image in the eyepiece.

4.7 Comma before <u>and</u> and other conjunctions

Comma before a co-ordinating <u>and</u>

In the general construction of sentences, since <u>and</u> is a co-ordinating signal, it is theoretically undesirable to have a comma (which is mainly a boundary-marker or a separating signal) immediately before it:

WRITE _____ and _____
NOT   _____, and _____

But in practice, <u>and</u> can be left to co-ordinate and balance two items only if the items are short, and if there is no possibility of momentary mis-reading or complete ambiguity. It is often good tactics to add a comma before <u>and</u> to make clear the logic, balance, or emphasis you require.

The items on each side of an <u>and</u> may be single words or larger word-groups. In the following examples, <u>and</u> co-ordinates single words or short word-groups; the statements are manageable and unambiguous:

Procedures must conform to existing standards and regulations.
(<u>and</u> co-ordinates two nouns)

... the two sentences can be co-ordinated and balanced ...
(<u>and</u> co-ordinates two adjectives)

... this system gives low picture distortion and a wide viewing angle.
(<u>and</u> co-ordinates two short phrases)

But as the word-groups joined by <u>and</u> become longer, readers find it helpful to receive a signal that one group has been completed, and the next group is about to begin:

WRITE The fission of the heavy elements can be provoked by neutral particles with energies of a few electron volts (eV), but the fusion of the light elements depends on bringing together two nuclei of the same charge, and if the Coulomb repulsive force between them is to be overcome successfully, the nuclei must be moving at high relative velocities ...

NOT   The fission of the heavy elements can be provoked by neutral particles with energies of a few electron volts (eV) but the fusion of the light elements depends on bringing together two nuclei of the same charge and if the Coulomb repulsive force between them is to be overcome successfully, the nuclei must be moving at high relative velocities ...

WRITE   Items serve as the nodes of the knowledge network, and user-defined relators serve as the links between items.

NOT   Items serve as the nodes of the knowledge network and user-defined relators serve as the links between items.

WRITE   A translator of technical texts often has to handle large amounts of information, and needs to ensure that it is stored in an easily retrievable form.

NOT   A translator of technical texts often has to handle large amounts of information and needs to ensure that it is stored in an easily retrievable form.

WRITE   The calculator executed the functions that had been selected, and displayed the results on the top half of the screen.

NOT   The calculator executed the functions that had been selected and displayed the results on the top half of the screen.

Unfortunately, it is not possible to say how long the co-ordinated word-groups can be before readers need the help of a boundary-marking comma. In my judgement, the next two examples do not need a comma:

The spectrophotometer is then 'zeroed' and the stopping syringe is emptied.

The flat terrain enabled the air-ground technique to be maximised and was a key factor in the achievement of rapid completion of the survey.

but the following two examples do:

More information is being made available to Department A from Department B, and Department C has been able to make more progress on completing modules.

The controller controls the burner sequences, and interfaces with the various plant interlocks and alarms.

As the previous two examples show, a comma is especially important if the word that completes the first large unit and the word that begins the second large unit *could* be interpreted as a co-ordinated pair (... from Department B and Department C ...; ... controls the burner sequences and interfaces ...). So I recommend that you follow the advice of *The Oxford Dictionary for Writers and Editors* 12th edition 1981 [p329], sadly omitted in the *New Oxford Dictionary for Writers and Editors* 2005, and insert a comma 'when, without the comma, the eye or tongue would run on and momentarily mistake the sense':

WRITE The processor accepts data from input devices, and checks it before computing ...

NOT The processor accepts data from input devices and checks it before computing ...

WRITE The species of fish supported by the reef are varied, and abundant food supplies are available to ...

NOT The species of fish supported by the reef are varied and abundant food supplies are available to ...

WRITE At high temperatures, all the ceramic materials show ductility, and hardness decreases considerably ...

NOT At high temperatures, all the ceramic materials show ductility and hardness decreases considerably ...

WRITE This produces hard copy that can be retained, but printed sheets are bulky to handle, so ...

NOT This produces hard copy that can be retained but printed sheets are bulky to handle, so ...

WRITE Connection to PTT-supplied packet-switch networks will be a prime requirement of the workstation, and gateways into these networks are planned by the PTTs ...

> NOT Connection to PTT-supplied packet-switch networks
> will be a prime requirement of the workstation and gate-
> ways into these networks are planned by the PTTs ...

Comma before _and_ in a list

When we have to present a list of items, we do not put _and_ repeat-
edly between the items; we put commas instead:

> NOT (Version 1) ... office equipment consists of a photocopier
> and a typewriter and a word processor and
> a printer and three filing cabinets ...
> BUT (Version 2) ... office equipment consists of a photocopier,
> a typewriter, a word processor, a printer
> and three filing cabinets ...

Conventional punctuation used to be as in Version 2, with a comma
in place of _and_ in all but the final position. The justification for this
convention was that commas were more economical signals than _ands_
throughout the list, but that it was useful to retain the final _and_ as
a signal that the final item in the list was about to arrive. Because
the commas were being used in place of _ands_, there was no need for a
comma before the final and: to put one would be unnecessary duplication. This was the basis of the English teachers' embargo on placing
a comma before _and_ that I mentioned in Part 1 (page 3).

However, this form of punctuation leads to trouble if the final item
in the list contains an _and_:

> WRITE ... the possibilities are error, repeat, and send and
> receive ...
> NOT ... the possibilities are error, repeat and send and
> receive ...

And here are two more examples of statements that would have been
at least momentarily misleading without a comma before _and_:

> ... stoppages have been due to fractures, omissions, incorrect
> sizing, and operating faults ...

... symptoms including obsessional compulsive behaviours, depression and anxiety, self-injurious behaviour, and aggression.

Accordingly, modern practice (supported, for example, by *New Hart's Rules* [p71] and *The Oxford Guide to Style* [p121]) is to supply a comma before the final <u>and</u>, to ensure that the itemisation is always absolutely clear:

(Version 3) ... office equipment consists of a photocopier, a type-writer, a word processor, a printer, and three filing cabinets ...

Certainly, there is still extensive debate about this practice. *Copy-Editing: the Cambridge Handbook* [p156] comments simply that:

A comma should be consistently omitted or included before the final 'and' or 'or' in lists of three or more items ...

and *The Economist Style Guide* [p116] says:

... with lists do not put a comma before *and* at the end of a sequence of items unless one of the items includes another *and*.

Collins Cobuild English Usage says firmly [p754]:

You must put a comma ... between items in a list, except ones separated by *and* or *or*

although it continues:

... when items are in a list, some writers also place a comma after the last item, before *and* or *or*

I commend to you the words of G. V. Carey in *Mind the Stop* [p65]:

When all is said, this remains a matter for individual choice. But it is also a matter of general principle; you can belong to the 'final comma school' or the 'no final comma school', but, having made your choice, you should aim at consistency. Because the 'no final comma' principle breaks down now and again through ambiguity, whilst the 'final comma' principle can be followed consistently with less risk of it, I personally vote for the latter.

I share Carey's view.

4.8 Comma after <u>that is</u>, <u>for example</u>, and <u>for instance</u>

Normally, put a comma after expressions such as <u>that is</u>, <u>for example</u>, and <u>for instance</u>, that 'extend' a previous statement:

> ... the help system in use at X, for instance, encourages users ...
> For instance, on a typical industrial-grade monitor, a common ...

> ... on a task he had not done before, that is, page layout.

> ... the trouble is in the interfaces. That is, each of the components ...

> ... are documents that have difficult-to-find information, for example, library card catalogues.

> ... can identify its ID by using the X command. For example, if you want to find ...

> ... it is named and enclosed in angle brackets: for example, <filename>, ...

> ... the audience's interaction with the text and the task at hand (for example, assembling the components of a personal computer system); ...

As the examples show, the punctuation *before* such expressions can vary widely, depending on how distinctly you want to set off the extending words from the preceding statement: that is, depending on the rhetorical effect you want to achieve.

A word of warning: always write out <u>that is</u> and <u>for example</u> in full, because many of your readers – even native speakers of English – will be unsure which of the Latin abbreviations i.e. and e.g. equates to each English phrase.

Note that the 'extending' expression <u>such as</u> is not normally followed by a comma.

4.9 Commas in numbers

In general, do NOT use a comma to indicate thousands or millions when you are writing numbers.

In its guide *How to Write Metric* [p23] the Metrication Board recommended that, except in writing sums of money:

- four digits should be written without a space, unless they form part of a tabulation;

- five or more digits should be grouped in blocks of three, divided by single spaces.

WRITE	3000,	30 000,	30 000 000
NOT	3,000,	30,000,	30,000,000

These rules, it said, should be applied consistently on both sides of the decimal marker:

WRITE	54 321.123 45
NOT	54,321.12345

The Board emphasised that a comma should not be used as a thousands marker, because it is used in some countries as a decimal marker. However, the exception for writing sums of money is justified by the possibility that a space might be filled fraudulently with another digit.

In *New Hart's Rules*, one of the principal guides used by professional writers, you are advised to insert commas in four or more figures in non-technical contexts [p182]; but in *scientific* work you are advised to write numbers up to 9999 closed up (without a comma), and to write numbers above 9999 with thin spaces after each group of three digits to the right or left of the decimal point [p261].

The best advice I can offer is that you or your organisation choose one set of conventions for expressing numbers, and keep to that set consistently.

For the use of a comma as a decimal marker, see section 8.4.

Dash: em rule (—) and en rule (–)

5.1 Em rules, en rules, and hyphens

Dashes come in two lengths: *em* dashes (or em rules) and *en* dashes (or en rules):

Em rule (a rule the length of a letter m) —
En rule (a rule the length of a letter n)   –

Em rules/dashes are separating signals; en rules/dashes are joining signals. Do not confuse *em* rules and *en* rules with hyphens:

Hyphen   -

Hyphens also are joining signals, used principally to join words into compounds (see full discussion in section 9).

5.2 Indicating a parenthetic remark

Use a pair of em dashes to set off heavy parenthetic 'asides':

... creating tensions between country-level bodies — ministries of health and national AIDS councils — over respective roles ...

... it is interesting to note that the aptamer binding theophylline — another small, planar, aromatic ligand — that we have studied previously ...

See also the discussion under commas in section 4.2.

5.3 Adding emphasis, afterthought, or final 'punch'

Use a single em dash to add a phrase or clause to a statement, especially to create a pause before a final 'punch' or emphatic statement at the end:

> ... consistently achieved 50 gallons per hour — optimum output.

> ... this can be done by omitting the additive — though this should be done only as a last resort.

5.4 Signalling a span or link

Use an en dash to signal a span or a link:

> ... on pages 45–53 ...
> ... the London–Amsterdam flight ...
> ... such as a Newton–Raphson algorithm ...
> ... the DNA–enzyme interactions ...
> ... has been done for the sucrose–water system ...
> ... longitudinal slip present at a rail–wheel contact ...

5.5 En dash as a minus sign

British Standard 5775: Part 0 : 1993 (ISO 31–0: 1992) [p11] specifies that the symbol for a unit should be placed after the numerical value in the expression for a quantity, leaving a space between the numerical value and the unit symbol (for example: 20.7 m), and adds that:

> It should be noted that, in accordance with this rule, the symbol °C for degree Celsius shall be preceded by a space when expressing a Celsius temperature ... [for example: 24.6 °C, not: 24.6°C].

It offers two possibilities for placing a common unit symbol when you use an en dash as a minus sign in a mathematical statement:

Height = 20.7 m – 7.2 m = 13.5 m
Height = (20.7 – 7.2) m = 13.5 m

5.6 Problems in typing or word-processing

When the earliest editions of this book were current, writers frequently faced problems because most typewriters and some word-processing systems did not provide different symbols for a hyphen, an em dash and an en dash. As a result, it was frequently necessary to use the same keyboard character, - , for all three. As I write this in 2006, most people are using word-processing programmes that provide all three symbols; but some word-processing programmes and e-mail systems still make available only a hyphen, and if you are not aware of that, the message you thought was clearly punctuated when it left you will look confusing when it arrives at its electronic destination.

If you have only the one symbol, - , available, make your text as clear as possible by NOT leaving character spaces each side of a *hyphen*:

> WRITE ... insert position-marking symbols ...
> NOT ... insert position - marking symbols ...

But DO leave character spaces each side of the symbol when you use it to represent an *en dash*:

> ... on pages 45-53 ...
>
> ... the London - Amsterdam flight ...
>
> ... using a Geiger - Muller counter ...

or an *em dash*:

> ... use dashes - inserted by typing Alt-0151 on the keypad - to mark the parenthesis.

Alternatively, type two hyphens *without* character spaces each side to represent an en dash, and two hyphens *with* character spaces each side to represent an em dash:

> ... the London--Amsterdam flight ...
>
> ... using dashes -- inserted by typing Alt-0150 on the keypad -- to mark the parenthesis.

The safest solution, where possible, is to re-word the statement you want to make.

5.7 Differing publishing-house conventions

Two more points need to be made in this new edition as a result of the passage of time: one is that few publishing-houses now put a character space on each side of an em dash; the other is that many publishing houses (including Routledge!) have begun to omit em dashes altogether.

Failure to put a character space on each side of an em dash closes up the text in a way that I think looks squashed, reducing the clarity of the signal that parenthetical or added information is about to appear:

> For this ambitious goal to be reached—from a base of fewer than 200,000 patients—countries, donors, and multilateral agencies must know ...

> a few MSSA isolates with ST36—corresponding to generic background C—were detected among historically ...

> ... you do not have to use the Subtotals command to summarise the results—the PivotTable report does that work for you.

> ... active orbit and attitude control, a new challenge is faced—cost-effective propulsion.

Publishers who use en dashes wherever they might previously have used em dashes do, at least, leave character spaces on each side of the dash, which emphasises the separation:

> ... the unemployed respondents were more likely to be in the manual group – 60% compared with 39% of the employed – although a further 10% ...

> ... the hopping robot of Thomson & Raibert has only springs but – as the authors point out themselves – its motion is not stable ...

> ... had 'airlock' – two sets of lockable doors positioned opposite each other ...

> ... patients on medium secure units – these had already been studied previously ...

However, the en dash is now being used for three purposes: to signal a parenthesis; to signal a link; and as a minus sign (as, for example, in $x - 5 = y$). It seems to me that there is a loss of discrimination in the use of the single symbol for three purposes. Frequently, as I read modern texts, I am obliged to pause momentarily to check that I am interpreting the signals correctly. So to give readers maximum visual help from my use of dashes, my practice is to use:

- em dashes with spaces on each side to mark parentheses and final emphases;

- en dashes with no separating character spaces to signal links;

- en dashes in front of numbers as minus signs.

But to mark parentheses and final emphases, the *Cambridge Guide to English Usage* and *The Economist Style Guide* use en dashes with character spaces on each side; the *Oxford Guide to Style* and the *Chicago Manual of Style* use em dashes without separating spaces.

What should you do? If you are preparing a text for a publisher, you must conform to the house style specified. If you have the opportunity to choose, once again the best advice I can offer is that you or your organisation choose one set of conventions for using dashes, and keep to that set consistently.

6

Ellipsis Points (...)

An ellipsis is an omission of one or more words from a sentence, usually from a sentence or paragraph you are quoting. Mark an ellipsis by three 'ellipsis points' – three dots, full stops, or periods set at normal character-spacing along a line of text:

> Changes in the media temperature ... do not affect the meter's performance.

> ... gives a total of 48 bits. However, ... a 24-bit card uses more than ...

> Each colour on your screen can be set to solid ..., transparent, or ...

An ellipsis may be at the beginning, middle, or end of a sentence, or between two complete sentences. To show an ellipsis at the end of a sentence, indicating that a *statement* was not finished, simply use three ellipsis points:

> The keyboard's main uses, for local operation and for programming, ...

To show an ellipsis at the end of a sentence, indicating that a *question* or an *exclamation* was not finished, put a question mark or exclamation mark after three ellipsis points:

> Would the operator be more comfortable with a tungsten uplight, an overhead fluorescent light, or ...?

To show the omission of one or more complete sentences from between two other complete sentences, precede the ellipsis points with the normal full stop (placed close to the final word) at the end of the first sentence, and follow them with a capital letter to signal that the subsequent words were the beginning of a new sentence:

> In earlier versions of X, all templates had to be saved with a file-name of up to eight characters. ... Now you can create categories for your templates ...

To show an ellipsis at the beginning of a sentence, precede three ellipsis points with the normal full stop (placed close to the final word) at the end of the previous sentence, and follow them with a lower-case letter to signal that the subsequent words were not the beginning of the next sentence:

> ... may be caused by the foetus moving. ... allow time for the signal to stabilise before you ...

If you add any words within an ellipsis to clarify the text, enclose your interpolation within square brackets:

> Avoid indiscriminate use of this word ... [while] ... Many writers use it frequently as a substitute for *and* or *but* ...

However, if you add a word or words within a quotation to make the meaning clearer, but you do not omit any words from the sentence, do NOT use ellipsis points: simply put your interpolation in square brackets:

> Information relating to this [operating] philosophy is presented in Volume 5, Chapter 6.

It is not essential to indicate the length of an ellipsis (that is, the number of words omitted). Three ellipsis points may be used to signal the omission of three words or thirty. But if you wish to show that the omitted text was lengthy, running at least from paragraph to paragraph, or even from page to page, put three ellipsis points to show the end of one paragraph or page, and three more to show that there is a substantial omission before you begin again:

> A WARNING should be given where failure to observe the instructions could result in injury to persons. ...

... A CAUTION should be given where failure to observe the instructions could result in damage to the product or pollution of another product.

If you use ellipsis points to signal omissions from a series of terms, ensure that other punctuation marks or mathematical signs appear in their normal places in the series:

WRITE $a_1, a_2, ..., a_n$
NOT $a_1, a_2, ...a_n$

WRITE $b_1 + b_2 + ... + b_n$
NOT $b_1 + b_2 + ... b_n$

Sometimes, ellipsis points are used to indicate that a list or enumeration of items could run on almost endlessly:

... permits an almost unlimited range of colour combinations: blue and yellow, blue and green, yellow and green, yellow and red, ...

Usually, this use of ellipsis points is equivalent to the use of etc (*et cetera* = 'and the rest', 'and similar things'):

The name of the robot in each cell is shown in parentheses: for example, (T1), (A4), (C1), ...

The name of the robot in each cell is shown in parentheses: for example, (T1), (A4), (C1), etc.

But use of either of these devices seems casual, implying 'I can't be bothered to write these things out in full', or 'There must be some more, but I can't think of them at the moment', so avoid such 'tailing off': give a firmer impression by using a statement such as:

The name of the robot in each cell is shown in parentheses: for example, (T1), (A4) and (C1).

Exclamation mark (!)

Generally, an exclamation mark (called an exclamation *point* in the USA) is used to express astonishment or surprise. In scientific and technical writing, you are unlikely to find many appropriate occasions to use one. But it is a legitimate signal, and can sometimes be used effectively to highlight a surprising fact or to reinforce a warning:

> ... note that cyanide solution and cyanide gas can cause severe poisoning simply by absorption through the skin. It is not enough just to avoid drinking the solution or inhaling the gas! Always wear the protective clothing listed in Section 3, and follow the operating instructions given in Section 4.

A special use of the exclamation mark is its use in mathematics to indicate a factorial (the product of all the positive integers from 1 to n), symbolised as $n!$. If you are using an exclamation mark in this special way in your text, avoid using the same mark to express astonishment or surprise, perhaps by using an expression such as 'It is surprising that ...' or 'Surprisingly, ...'

Full Stop (.)

8.1 Marking the end of a sentence

The principal use of the full stop or full point (called a *period* in the USA) is to signal the end of a declarative or imperative sentence (that is, a sentence that makes a statement or that issues an instruction):

... The mask temperature fluctuates throughout the experiment. (declarative)

... Align the three holes in the steering-assembly shaft with the three holes in the handle-assembly collar. (imperative)

Use a full stop also after a parenthetic statement that forms a complete sentence between other sentences:

... for the last two batches, we have used a gravimetric method for trace analysis. (The method is described in Internal Report No. 67.) This method gives results that are ...

8.2 Marking titles, abbreviations and acronyms

Do NOT use full stops:

• after titles, headings, and sub-headings;

• after units:

WRITE cm, in, kg, kHz,
NOT cm., in., kg., kHz.

- within capitalised abbreviations or acronyms:

WRITE VDU, MTBF, USA, UK, NATO,
NOT V.D.U., M.T.B.F., U.S.A., U.K., N.A.T.O.

Use full stops between letters in lower-case abbreviations. Do not use e.g. and i.e. at all (see pages 51 and 101):

... the e.s.r. spectrum (electron-spin-resonance spectrum)
... the r.f. output (radio-frequency output) ...
... to cover the visible and u.v. (ultra-violet) ranges ...

Use full stops after abbreviations formed by truncation (cutting off the end of the word), except after abbreviations of units:

WRITE No.; Fig.; Sun.; Mon.; Jan.; Feb.

In correspondence, use a full stop after an abbreviation of a personal title or of a place name, except when the abbreviation contains the first and last letters of the abbreviated word:

Prof., Dr, Mr, Mrs
Co., Ltd
Pl. (Place), Sq. (Square), Rd (Road), St (Street)

In correspondence, the contracted form of the words Public Limited Company is sometimes written in capitals without internal stops and sometimes without a final stop:

EITHER ... to Someco PLC ...
OR ... to Someco P.L.C. ...

Once again, my main advice is that you should be consistent. Abandon the guidelines given in this section if your organisation's house style differs from the advice given here. The most important feature of these uses of full stops should be consistency within any organisation, preferably in conformity to international standards.

8.3 Full stop as a 'dot'

In computing, a full stop is often included as part of a command or a filename:

```
A command: C>prnt\autoexec.run
A filename: A:REPORT.DOC
```

In these uses, the full stop is placed on the line, as shown in the examples above. In discussion, both in speech and in writing, the mark is usually called a *dot*, not a full point, full stop, or period.

8.4 Full stop as a decimal marker

In Britain and the USA, a full stop is the conventional decimal marker. The marker may be placed as a mid-point (6·5, technically 'half-high') or on the line (6.5), though modern practice is usually to print it on the line.

Unfortunately, conventional practice in Britain and the USA does not conform to international standards. *British Standard 5775: Part 0: 1993*, which is identical to ISO (International Organization for Standardization) 31: Part 0, 1992 states [p11]:

> The decimal sign is a comma on the line.

but it acknowledges the different usage in documents written in English:

> NOTE 17 In documents in the English language, a dot is often used instead of a comma. If a dot is used, it should be on the line. In accordance with an ISO Council decision, the decimal sign is a comma in ISO documents.

If you are writing a document in English for international distribution without translation, you can consider producing different versions for different audiences; but that can cause confusion if a document designed for distribution in Scandinavia, using a comma as the decimal marker, comes into the hands of a reader in the UK or the USA. Most organisations in Britain and the USA rely on audiences recognising that a text written in English is following British or US conventions. Translators are given the job of converting the expression of decimal numbers at the same time as they convert the rest of the text into another language. However, if you think your audience may be confused by your conventions for showing decimals, put a note about those conventions somewhere at the start of your document.

8.5 Full stop as a multiplication sign

British Standard 5775: Part 0 [p11] states:

> The sign for multiplication of numbers is a cross (x) or a dot half-high.

It goes on to recommend [Notes 18 and 19, p11] that:

> If a dot half-high is used as the multiplication sign, a comma should be used as the decimal sign. If a dot is used as the decimal sign, a cross should be used as the multiplication sign. In ISO documents, the dot is not used directly between numbers to indicate multiplication.

As always, consistency is the key principle to follow.

8.6 Full stop after numbers and letters in lists, and after headings and side-headings

It is usual to include full stops after numbers and letters in lists:

1.	a. ....
2.	b. ....
3.	c. ....

but it is not usual to include full stops after headings or side-headings:

2   PUNCTUATION
2.1 Use of commas

However, this is more a matter of format than of punctuation, so once again, my main advice is that you and/or your organisation should be consistent in using or not using full stops in these situations.

Hyphen (-)

9.1 Linking words to form compounds

The hyphen is a *joining* signal, in contrast to an em dash, which is a separator (see section 5 for discussion of dashes). Its main use is to link two or more words together to form a compound adjective (or compound modifier) to describe (qualify or modify) another word:

a valve
a flow valve
a return valve
a flow-and-return valve

a scale
a nine-point scale
a nine-point, assessment-of-noise scale

a report
an occurrence report
an abnormal report
an abnormal-occurrence report

high-pressure chamber
slow-moving vehicle
primary-care clinic
hard-gel formulation
three-to-one ratio
up-and-over door
time-to-event analyses

As is discussed in section 4.5, if you intend each of several adjectives in a sequence *separately* to modify a noun, you need no hyphens. Simply help your reader by separating the adjectives with commas:

> ... an elastic, coated beam ...
> ... a single, scalar variable ...

But if you intend two or more words to form a compound to modify a noun, use one or more hyphens to signal the compound:

> ... is made of plastic-coated metal ...
> ... uses a single-word index to ...
> ... Xs are larger-than-usual units ...
> ... where Pap-smear-based screening is available ...

However, if you frequently link two or three words with hyphens to form pre-modifying units, as in the last two examples, it is probable that you will create an uncomfortable, 'lumpy' text. Preferably, re-construct your statement:

> ... Xs are larger units than usual ...
> ... where screening based on Pap smears is available ...

There is a conventional departure from this rule: you do not need to put commas after number adjectives and colour adjectives when you use them in combination with other modifiers, *provided* that there is no possibility of the number adjective or colour adjective being misinterpreted as part of a compound:

> ... three unused diskettes ...
> ... the red screw-topped container ...
> ... two reliable transmitters ...
> ... is decoded using the two frame-duration bits in each speech frame ...

But when the number or colour *is* intended as part of a compound, a hyphen is vital:

> ... two-part polyurethane compounds ...
> ... an unaffected silver-backed plate ...

There is often an interesting difference of meaning intended in three-word groups that consist of two adjectives in front of a noun. Most frequently, the two adjectives modify the noun individually, and (as described in section 4.5) it is helpful to signal that fact by separating the adjectives with commas:

> ... using separate, programmable units ...

Occasionally, however, the first word modifies the idea expressed by the second and third together:

> ... the failed primary controller ...

Here, the intended meaning is 'the primary controller that has failed', not 'the failed primary-controller'. Conventionally, when two adjectives appear before a noun in this way, and the first modifies the idea expressed by the second modifier and the noun combined, no hyphen or comma is used:

> ... your normal daily procedure ...
> ... the received analogue input ...

Use 'suspended' hyphens to create compounds in which two or more adjectives or numbers are attached to one other word:

WRITE ... percentage reduction is critical: over- and under-reduction cause the ink to be very ...

NOT ... percentage reduction is critical: over and under reduction cause the ink to be very ...

WRITE ... a realistic strategy in the design of both paper- and screen-based forms ...

NOT ... a realistic strategy in the design of both paper and screen based forms ...

WRITE ... 20-, 80-, and 100-ml containers ...
NOT ... 20, 80, and 100 ml containers ...

WRITE ... Morphological studies of paraquat- or oxygen-toxicity in rats have shown ...

NOT ... Morphological studies of paraquat or oxygen toxicity in rats have shown ...

But do not write:

> ... could use both non- and destructive testing methods ...

write:

> ... could use both destructive and non-destructive testing methods ...

However, interpretation of structures using suspended hyphens may be difficult for some readers working in English as their second or third language, and it is wise to re-word your thoughts if you can do so comfortably:

NOT ... involves judicious water and heat management strategies ...

PREFER ... involves judicious water- and heat-management strategies ...

BEST ... involves judicious strategies for managing water and heat ...

NOT ... because they eliminate model and method dependent scaling factors ...

PREFER ... because they eliminate model- and method-dependent scaling factors ...

BEST ... because they eliminate scaling factors that depend on the model and the method ...

A word of warning: remember to supply a hyphen when you want to create a compound consisting of a noun plus an -*ing* word-form. As our eyes and minds arrive at the sequence of words 'men behaving badly', our expectations about normal word-sequences in English lead us to interpret <u>men</u> as the subject of the group, <u>behaving</u> as the verb telling us what they are doing, and <u>badly</u> as an adverb telling us about the way they are behaving. Similarly, when we arrive at 'librarians seeking information', normal expectations lead us to interpret <u>librarians</u> as the subject of the group, <u>seeking</u> as the verb, and <u>information</u> as the object they are seeking. Because of normal expectations, the following hyphen-less sequences create images in our minds that disturb, albeit only momentarily, readers' concentration on the discourse of the text.

... bacteria carrying dust particles ...
... acetone carrying pipework ...
... breeding animals in nickel containing cages ...
... information seeking bahaviour ...
... heavy metal containing pigments ...
... is included to cover beta-lactamase producing anaerobes ...

Advice on how to write compounds is straightforward while we are considering adjectival compounds created from two or more independent *words*: write them with hyphens in between:

... spring-loaded ...
... dust-free ...
... heat-conducting ...

But conventions are not so easy to state when we consider how to write adjectival compounds formed by adding a prefix or suffix to a word, or when we consider how to write compound nouns or verbs. Certainly, prefixes and suffixes must not be left to stand alone:

WRITE	NOT
anti-irritant	anti irritant
pre-formed	pre formed
semi-conducting	semi conducting
multi-sectioned	multi sectioned
threadless	thread less
paper-less	paper less
OR paperless	

WRITE ... a toilet with a separate gravity-fed, non-potable wash-water system ...
NOT ... a toilet with a separate gravity fed non potable wash water system ...

WRITE ... is fitted with a small non-heat-conductive knob ...
NOT ... is fitted with a small non heat conductive knob ...

WRITE ... the non-return valve is screwed into the outlet port. The valve consists of a spring-loaded plunger and a ...
NOT ... the non return valve is screwed into the outlet port. The valve consists of a spring loaded plunger and a ...

But beyond that, rules describing modern usage are difficult to state. Compound adjectives (and compound nouns and verbs) are commonly written in three ways:

- open (a check list, a data base, to down load, to drip feed);

- hyphened (a disk-drive, a data-base, to down-load, to drip-feed);

- solid (an update, a database, to download, to dripfeed).

In general, we gradually 'close' pairs of words as they become used together with increasing frequency. At first, the pairing is just an occasional use of an adjective and a noun:

... a motor cycle ...

Gradually, the pair is used more regularly as a single unit, and we signal that fact by insertion of a hyphen:

... a motor-cycle ...

Eventually, the unit is regularly thought of as a single entity, and we reflect that in the way we write the word:

... a motorcycle ...

But we are inconsistent in the signalling of the increased closeness. We write either <u>under-estimate</u> or <u>underestimate</u>, but never <u>under-take</u>.

However, three broad generalisations are possible:

- if you form compound adjectives by adding words ending in <u>ing</u> or <u>ed</u> to another word, the compound should usually be hyphened (fuel-containing, load-carrying, high-geared, dark-adjusted, walking-aid, breaking-strain, ignition-producing);

- though you may sometimes write a compound *noun* in open form (short circuit, steady state), your reader will need the help of a hyphen in that compound when you use it as an adjective (short-circuit signal, steady-state operation);

- if you add a prefix to a proper noun (name) or to any word beginning with a capital letter, you should use a hyphen (anti-British, post-Mendelian, a pre-TR cell, pro-Newton argument).

Remember the principle stated on page 8: the onus for reducing uncertainty lies on the writer, not on the reader. Do not require your readers to work out that <u>stationary focus spectrum recording</u> means 'stationary-focus spectrum-recording'; that <u>morpholine containing effluent</u> means 'morpholine-containing effluent'; or that <u>multiple rat cages</u> means 'multiple-rat cages'. Supply clear guides to rapid and comfortable reading.

9.2 Using hyphens to avoid ambiguity

Write solid (closed up, without a hyphen) most compounds formed by adding a prefix to a full word: <u>reconsider</u>, <u>unfasten</u>, <u>subroutine</u>; but use a hyphen if there is any likelihood that readers will mis-read a solid compound because of its unfamiliarity or ambiguity. In particular, use hyphens to create most compounds in which the prefix ends with a vowel and the root word begins with a vowel:

de-energise
re-elect
pre-amplifier
re-adjust
re-enter
de-activate
de-ice

Some writers nowadays feel that this separation of vowels is old-fashioned and unnecessary. They point out that words such as <u>cooperate</u>, <u>coordinate</u>, and <u>reiterate</u> are commonly written solid, and argue that other words with two vowels together could be written likewise.

No doubt, frequent daily use would lead to the acceptance of solid versions of words such a <u>reelect</u>, <u>reenter</u>, <u>preeminent</u>, <u>preecho</u>, or <u>deicing</u>; but most readers do not meet such words regularly, and when they see <u>reelect</u> or <u>preeminent</u>, they are surprised. Certainly, they need only a moment to adjust the way they 'pronounce' the pairs of vowels, but the need for even momentary adjustments disturbs their concentration on the over-all meaning of the text.

Regrettably, there is no reliable rule I can give for which prefixed words should be hyphened and which should be written solid. Most British writers write <u>non-stop</u> and <u>non-standard</u> but <u>nonconformity</u>

and <u>noncommittal</u>. Most British writers use hyphens in words beginning with <u>quasi</u>, but write words beginning with <u>anti</u> solid.

My own practice is conservative. I think it is worth helping readers recognise *instantly* when <u>rea ...</u> is to be 'heard' as a single syllable (*ree*, as in <u>reach</u> or <u>readability</u>), and when it is to be heard as two syllables (*ree + a* as in <u>re-activate</u> or <u>re-administer</u>). I acknowledge, though, that I write <u>react</u> and <u>readmit</u> solid. I decide whether or not to use a hyphen by estimating the probability of readers being surprised and distracted by a solid version of the word.

An alternative way to show that the second of a pair of vowels is intended as a separate syllable is to use a diaeresis – two dots over a vowel, as in the 'old-fashioned' spelling of naïve. But a diaeresis is rarely seen nowadays, and would probably bewilder more readers than it would help, so a hyphen is the best signal we have to help our readers see *immediately* how to read the syllables in words such as <u>antiicing</u> (anti-icing), <u>antiinflammatory</u> (anti-inflammatory), <u>coedit</u> (co-edit), <u>deactivate</u> (de-activate), <u>deamination</u> (de-amination), <u>deenergise</u> (de-energise), and <u>preeclampsia</u> (pre-eclampsia).

I think it is fair to say that the insertion of a hyphen will rarely confuse: omission of a hyphen may often do so. But be consistent in your use of hyphens to avoid misleading or puzzling forms. Especially, when two or more writers or editors work as a team, it is desirable to establish an agreed list of prefixed compounds that will normally be hyphened.

9.3 Miscellaneous special cases

Use hyphens to create compounds that could be confused with other words spelt similarly, but with different meaning (homographs):

```
    re-form : reform
re-creation : recreation
 re-collect : recollect
   re-cover : recover
```

Use hyphens to create compounds in which a misleading or awkward combination of consonants would be formed by joining the words:

```
animal-like        de-stabilise
hyper-renanaemic   mis-shapen
```

mis-spell	post-transplantation
short-term	water-repellent

Note, however, that <u>withhold</u> is usually written solid.

Use hyphens when you create compounds that consist of a capital letter and a noun:

I-beam rafter
T-square measurement
four U-beams

Use hyphens when you create compound verbs that consist of a noun plus a verb:

to die-cast
to arc-weld
to field-test

Use hyphens when you have to write out two-word fractions or numbers, or if you have to use fractions that are not on your keyboard (but preferably use decimal notations in those circumstances):

forty-seven
ninety-ninth
one hundred and sixty-two
three-sixteenths
one thirty-second
one-half
8-1/12
8-4/5

9.4 Exceptions to the general use of hyphens

Five exceptions to the general use of hyphens in compound adjectives are:

• usually leave open any compounds acting as adjectives in which a number is preceded by a plus, a minus or a plus-or-minus sign:

... connected to the +28 volt battery terminal ...

- usually leave open any compounds you use to complete the verb <u>to be</u>:

      ... the door is wide open ...
      ... the tools are well designed ...

- usually leave open any compounds formed from an adverb ending in <u>-ly</u> followed by an adjective:

      ... an extremely important matter ...
      ... a finely adjusted gauge ...

- DO NOT use hyphens to create compound words out of chemical compounds:

      ... carbon monoxide poisoning ...
      ... methyl bromide solution ...

- DO NOT use hyphens to create compounds of three words in which the first two words are adverbs:

      ... a very well defined area ...
      ... an unusually badly written program ...

9.5 A postscript on style and the use of hyphens

In this section (section 9), I have advocated the use of hyphens and commas as a means of organising multiple modifiers (adjectives) in front of nouns. However, I should like to emphasise a point I made in section 9.1: as a matter of style, long strings of modifiers before nouns are undesirable, with or without hyphens. These 'adjectival seaserpents', as H. W. Fowler calls them in *Modern English Usage* [p257], are difficult for readers to absorb:

      ... a mobile hopper fed compressed air operated grit blasting machine ...

      ... using a pressure sensitive low temperature curing glasscloth coating varnish ...

Often, too, they are ambiguous:

> ... a complex frequency error correction procedure ...
>
> ... system for automatic land vehicle monitoring ...

Certainly, they become easier to read when punctuation is added, but they are still awkward, unnatural English. It is unwise to try to save a clumsily written sentence by inserting several hyphens. A basic principle of good technical writing is to re-distribute the modifiers around the noun, as we would in normal, non-technical English:

> WRITE ... a mobile grit-blasting machine, fed from a hopper, and operated by compressed air ...
> NOT ... a mobile, hopper-fed, compressed-air-operated, grit-blasting machine ...

> WRITE ... using a glasscloth-coating varnish that is sensitive to pressure, and cures at low temperature ...
> NOT ... a pressure-sensitive, low-temperature-curing, glass-cloth-coating varnish ...

> WRITE ... a complex procedure for correcting frequency errors ...
> NOT ... a complex frequency-error-correction procedure ...

> WRITE ... system for automatic monitoring of land vehicles ...
> NOT ... system for automatic land-vehicle-monitoring ...

Also as a matter of style, occasionally break any of the 'rules' in this section (section 9) if you feel that you would cause ambiguity or discomfort by conforming to them rigidly. For example, it would be wise writing to put a hyphen in the statement <u>Normally-closed contacts 3 and 6 connect the anode to ...</u>, because strict observance of the rule about adverbs ending in <u>-ly</u> might lead a reader to mis-read the text to mean 'Normally, closed contacts 3 and 6 connect the anode to ...'.

As you write, bear in mind two main principles: that a hyphen is a *joining* signal (not a separator, like a dash), and that you are likely to help your reader by using too many rather than too few hyphens.

Perhaps you have been advised to cut out hyphens. Here is such advice – the considered judgement of Christine Browning, author of *Guide to Effective Software Technical Writing* [p83]:

Hyphenation is spelled c-l-u-t-t-e-r.

She comments that 'hyphens have been dying for years', and supports her case with this reasoning:

> Hyphens are real troublemakers in an automated text processing environment. Whenever you hyphenate unnecessarily, you are causing extra work for the typesetter. Machines and their operators have enough trouble handling hyphenation at the end of the line without having to contend with extraneous hyphens running through the text.

I cannot see why a hyphen calls for more work from a compositor or typesetter than a space. But I am mainly disturbed that an adviser on effective writing should reject hyphens in their main use just because some machine-operators have trouble remembering how to deal with word-division. Dividing or breaking words is a different activity from creating compounds. It is unhelpful (to put it mildly!) to confuse the two.

For the use of hyphens in word-division, see Appendix 2, pages 115 to 118.

Inverted Commas (or Quotation Marks)

Single (' ') or Double (" ")

10.1 Single or double?

In 1906, the lexicographers and grammarians H. W. and E. G. Fowler wrote in *The King's English* [p296]:

> There are single and double quotation-marks, and ... two ways of utilizing the variety. The prevailing one is to use double marks for most purposes, and single ones for quotations within quotations. ... The more logical method is that adopted, for instance, by the Oxford University Press, of reserving the double marks exclusively for quotations within quotations ...

In modern usage, there is still variation; but it is possible to generalise by saying that the most common usage in British English (advocated by *New Hart's Rules* [p85] and by *Copy-Editing: the Cambridge Handbook* [p264]) is to use single as the norm, and to use double only when you want to include a quotation or an emphasised word within a quotation. The most common practice in American English usage (advocated by *The Chicago Manual of Style* [p453] and by *Merriam-Webster's Manual for Writers and Editors* [p31]) is to use double as the norm, and to use single for quotations or emphasised words within quotations.

As in so many of the guidelines in this book, I have to recommend principally that you or your organisation choose one convention, and keep to it consistently.

10.2 Enclosing direct quotations

Use inverted commas to enclose short, direct quotations:

> ... the standard states: 'Upper-case letters in diagrams should be at least 1.6 mm high' ...

> ... In the opinion of Mary Smith: 'The possibility of introducing this agent into the adjuvant setting, and the introduction of new combinations, doses, and schedules remain exciting options' ...

The appropriate way of setting out a quotation depends on its length, and on how distinctly you wish to separate the quotation from your own words in a statement.

A long quotation should be set as a 'display' – as an inset section within or completing your own paragraph, preceded by a colon, as is this quotation about quotation marks from *A Comprehensive Grammar of the English Language* [p1630]:

> Quotation marks may be single '...' or double "...". The latter are more usual in handwritten and typed material and in American printing; the former are more usual in British printing, but the choice lies principally with individual printing houses.

If you wish to quote only a short group of words, using them as an intrinsic part of your own sentence, no preceding mark is usually necessary:

> The consultant's report describes the gravity sewer as 'seriously undersized', but suggests ...

If you wish to quote a full sentence, normally precede it with a comma:

> The customer's response was, 'If there is more than one day's delay, I shall cancel the contract'. We therefore invited him to ...

If, however, you want to throw particular emphasis on the formality or weight of the quotation, precede it with a colon:

X and Y now state in their latest paper (1987): 'There is a highly significant incidence of eye irritations, mucous-membrane symptoms, and headaches'. This changes their position substantially, so ...

When a quotation or an emphasised word or phrase completes a sentence, normally put the punctuation mark for the containing sentence *outside* the inverted commas:

WRITE The crucial words in the specification are 'the signals must be routed internally'.
  NOT The crucial words in the specification are 'the signals must be routed internally.'

WRITE Select the sub-function 'Create Unit Operation'.
  NOT Select the sub-function 'Create Unit Operation.'

WRITE We were unable to answer the question 'Why did the vat overflow?'.
  NOT We were unable to answer the question 'Why did the vat overflow?'

Considerable heat is generated in publishing houses and technical publications groups in debates about the placing of punctuation after parentheses and inverted commas at the ends of sentences. Broadly speaking, one school of thought argues that we should be guided by neatness, and advocates that all completing marks should go inside the final parenthesis or inverted comma, irrespective of meaning. For example:

... achieves what has been described as a 'substantial reduction in the crew's workload.'

The other school argues that the sole criterion for placing marks should be the showing up of logic or meaning. Accordingly, since the quoted words are only *part* of the sentence, the full stop should be placed outside the final inverted comma:

... achieves what has been described as a 'substantial reduction in the crew's workload'.

I believe it is best in scientific and technical work to make the showing up of logic and meaning your main motive for placing marks, and my advice at the beginning of this section is based on that belief; but to follow that advice slavishly could lead to the production of a text such as:

> What answer could we give to XYZ Company's question: 'How long will it be before the equipment can be left unattended?'?

Strict logic requires a question mark on each side of the final inverted comma; but even supporters of the logical school admit the clumsy appearance of such a text, and they are usually prepared to concede that logic should give way to appearance in such a case.

However, such an utterance is much more likely to occur in speech than in writing. I have never seen such a text, and cannot imagine a real-life circumstance in which it might seem a necessary piece of technical writing. If you find yourself confronted by the apparent need to use punctuation marks in the way shown in that theoretical example, heed the Fowler brothers' advice in *The King's English* [p292]:

> ... the right substitute for correct ugliness is not incorrect prettiness, but correct prettiness. There is never any difficulty in rewriting sentences like these.

The theoretical utterance, in a written text, might be revised to:

> EITHER We have still to answer XYZ Company's question: 'How long will it be before the equipment can be left unattended?'.
>
> OR XYZ Company's question, 'How long will it be before the equipment can be left unattended?' has still to be answered.

10.3 Giving extra stress to a word or phrase

Use inverted commas to focus attention on a word or phrase:

> ... is known as an 'escape character' ...
> ... the increase is described as 'moderate' when it is ...
> ... these areas, or 'fields', are outlined in ...
> ... such a 'user-friendly' program brings great advantages ...

We use inverted commas in this way for two purposes:

1. to focus attention on a word or phrase we want readers to note and/or learn;

2. to indicate to readers a querying, sceptical tone we would introduce if we were using the word or phrase in speech.

In each of the following three examples, the writer is introducing a new term, and wants us to note and/or learn it:

> ... called the 'contours from green principle' ...
> (the writer is introducing a new term, and wishes to highlight it, to encourage readers to remember it)

> ... this is known as the 'intermediary code' between ...
> (the writer is introducing a new term, and wishes to highlight it, to encourage readers to remember it)

> ... is a 'concomitant' or accompanying response ...
> (the writer recognises that <u>concomitant</u> is archaic or over-formal, but wants to include it because it is a word that is used by other writers; to be helpful, he supplies a synonym, <u>accompanying</u>, as well, to make the meaning clear)

In each of the following three examples, the writer wants to signal a special overtone to his/her statement:

> ... this 'automatic' selection requires the operator to ...
> (the writer wants to indicate that <u>automatic</u> is being used in a special way; often, this use of inverted commas signals scepticism – that the writer thinks the word is not really appropriate for the use that someone else has made of it)

> ... these 'new' files, which in reality have been changed only by the addition of ...
> (the writer is conscious that the use of <u>new</u> may not seem apt to all readers, but wants it accepted to express meaning approximately for the time being; it is important that the meaning implied by this use of inverted commas should be clear from the context)

Although bromobutyl and chlorobutyl rubbers have been available for more than ten years, they are still considered 'modern' polymers in this field.
(the writer wishes to indicate that the term <u>modern</u> is widely used, but in her opinion it is not really appropriate)

Now that modern word-processing equipment has made the use of italics and bolding widely available, it is often convenient to use italics or bolding to signal that you want readers to note and/or learn a word or phrase, and to reserve the use of inverted commas to signal special overtones to your statement.

Occasionally, also, we use inverted commas to signal a 'characteristic' rather than an actual quotation:

... Social workers often meet a 'Don't you tell me what's good for me' attitude among the clients who ...

As you read that comment within inverted commas, no doubt you heard in 'your mind's ear' the querulous tone that typically would accompany the comment in speech. You interpreted the rhetorical intention of the inverted commas.

10.4 Indicating chapter titles

Inverted commas are used conventionally by publishing houses to indicate titles of chapters in books and of articles in journals:

... should read G. V. Carey's chapter 'Proof Correction' in *Mind the Stop*.

Titles of books and journals are normally in italic type. See section 16.3 for points on the use of italic type.

Parentheses (or Brackets) ( )

11.1 Variations in terminology

Before describing the use of parentheses, I must alert you to the variations of terminology used to discuss this topic. There are differences between common usage and professional usage, and differences between usage in British English and usage in American English.

In common usage in Britain, we use the term *brackets* for (.....), *square brackets* for [.....], and *angle brackets* for <.....>; but printers and some other professional groups (notably mathematicians and computer specialists) use the term *parentheses* for (.....), *square brackets* or just *brackets* for [.....], and *angle brackets* for <.....>.

In the USA, (.....) are *parentheses*, [.....] are *brackets*, and <.....> are *angle brackets*.

The 'curly brackets' that group items in tabulations or lists, {.....}, are officially called *braces* in both British English and American English.

For scientific and technical writing in Britain, I recommend that you get into the habit of using the term *parentheses* for (.....), *square brackets* for [.....], *angle brackets* for <.....>, and *braces* for {.....}.

Scientific and technical readers in Britain will interpret the term *parentheses* reliably, even if their English teachers in school always used the term *brackets*. All readers in the USA will interpret *parentheses* reliably without special thought.

I recommend the term *square brackets* for [.....] because that term is understood immediately in Britain, and American readers will recognise without difficulty what it means. In contrast, if you use the term *brackets* for [.....], you may mislead some of your British readers.

The term *angle brackets* for <.....> will be understood without difficulty by all scientific and technical readers.

The term *braces* may be unfamiliar to some readers on both sides of the Atlantic; so if you need to write about braces rather than just use them, help your readers by adding the explanation 'curly brackets' in parentheses in your text, or better still by illustrating braces in parentheses.

The use of parentheses and brackets in the presentation of mathematical, chemical, and other scientific work is complex, and the conventions used in publishing houses differ. *New Hart's Rules* [p281] (Oxford University Press) says the sequence of brackets in mathematical formulae should be {[(.....)]}. *Copy-Editing* [p310] (Cambridge University Press) agrees, but adds:

> ... but it is unlikely to be worth changing a consistent system so long as it is one of different kinds of brackets.

In computing and other subjects, different kinds of brackets are used to symbolise precise meanings. So the main advice I can give on the use of parentheses and brackets as part of mathematical or scientific nomenclature is that you and/or your organisation choose one system and use it consistently, preferably conforming to the most-used conventions in your science or technology.

11.2 Enclosing parenthetic remarks

Fortunately, the use of parentheses in normal prose text is not so complex, and conventions differ little between British English and American English.

The principal use of parentheses is to mark the boundaries of an 'aside' or extra remark within a statement. (*Parenthesis* comes from the Greek word meaning 'word or words added within or beside your main thesis'. The term has become used to describe *both* the marks used to signal the 'intrusion' *and* the content they enclose: we put parentheses around our parentheses!)

We use parentheses as just one way of showing the boundaries of a parenthetic remark inserted in a sentence. Depending on the 'depth' of the aside (or distance of the topic of the additional remark from the topic of the main sentence), we mark its boundaries with a pair of commas, a pair of parentheses, or a pair of dashes. Examples are given in the discussion of commas, section 4.2.

If you use parentheses to enclose an inserted remark, the parentheses mark the boundaries of the 'intrusion' into the sentence. You do not need additional punctuation:

> WRITE ... the glass content of this material is low (10% by weight) for this application ...
> NOT ... the glass content of this material is low, (10% by weight), for this application ...

> WRITE ... the animals will be fed with water (via an automatic system) *ad libitum* ...
> NOT ... the animals will be fed with water, (via an automatic system), *ad libitum* ...

However, note that parentheses may come immediately before or after another punctuation mark, and it is sometimes correct to have two or three punctuation marks in sequence:

> ... these paints had a 'pail life' (that is, usable life after mixing) of 200 minutes ...

> ... on a laboratory roller mill (diameter 20 cm), which produced ...

> ... the units produced by Someco are profiled (corrugated), which makes them unsuitable for ...

> ... would like to use material X but we cannot do so because it cannot be obtained in Birmingham (the client insists that it be obtained 'on a local basis'). ...

If you put a complete sentence as a parenthesis between two other complete sentences, put the full stop for the enclosed sentence *inside* the closing parenthesis:

> ... for the last two batches, we have used a gravimetric method for trace analysis. (The method is described in Internal Report No. 67.) This method gives results that are ...

11.3 Referring to tables and figures

Use parentheses as one way of referring to tables and figures:

... our plot of energy migration (Figure 2) shows the ...

11.4 Explaining acronyms

Use parentheses to enclose explanations of acronyms formed from groups of words, if you are going to use *the acronym* throughout your text:

... decision was taken to use GRP (glass-reinforced plastic). Two suppliers of GRP have been ...

... will be kept in the SPF (specific-pathogen-free) Unit and will be transferred to the animals when needed. Within the SPF Unit, ...

Use parentheses to enclose the acronym formed from groups of words, if you are going to use *the words* throughout your text:

... diets are based on Porton Combined Diet (PCD). Although Porton Combined Diet is not usually ...

However, if you intend to use *the words* throughout your text, ask yourself if it is really necessary to introduce the acronym.

11.5 Enclosing interpolations within square brackets

The main use for square brackets in prose text is to mark interpolations (usually words added by a writer or editor within a quotation) to emphasise that those words were not a part of the original text:

... is illustrated by his [Mandelbrot's] theoretical treatment of Zipf's 'law' ...

... the nth ordinates of the ... [simultaneous] ... wave-forms ...

11.6 Enclosing a parenthetic remark within a parenthetic remark

Occasionally, you may want to enclose a parenthetic remark within a parenthetic remark. You can do this by using commas, parentheses, dashes, or even (to avoid having round brackets within round brackets) square brackets:

> ... (though if any one person [a receiver] should read them all, a millionfold redundancy would exist) ...

The appropriate form depends, as discussed in section 4.2, on the 'depth' of the departure from the main statement. But before you use *any* signals to enclose parenthetic remarks within parenthetic remarks, ask yourself if it is really desirable to require your readers to recognise and assimilate so many layers of information. Usually, you will produce a more readable text by re-constructing your statement than by using complex embedding of parenthetic remarks within parenthetic remarks.

Question Mark (?)

12.1 Indicating the end of a direct question

The principal use of a question mark is to indicate the end of a direct question. Direct questions are particularly effective in documents that hold a 'dialogue' with readers:

... Does a fault vector exist?

- Yes: ...
- No: ...

12.2 Expressing doubt

A question mark can also be used to express doubt:

... results suggest that these cells are normal (?) and that ...
... requires an increase of 40% (or more?) before ...

However, in scientific and technical writing, it is probably more appropriate to express doubt by using words such as <u>perhaps</u> or <u>possibly</u>, or by re-wording the statement completely.

12.3 Expressing a polite request

In correspondence, we sometimes want to make a polite request, which seems like a question. Normally, such a request is NOT followed by a question mark:

WRITE Would you please supply a list of the correct settings for the ABC.

NOT   Would you please supply a list of the correct settings
for the ABC?

But a genuine *enquiry* should be followed by a question mark:

Would it be possible to increase our order from 70 to 120 units?

Semi-Colon (;)

13.1 Co-ordinating related statements within a sentence

Use a semi-colon to link statements that are grammatically independent but are too closely related in meaning to be separated by a full stop.

The semi-colon is a heavier stop than a comma, but lighter than a full stop. It is a co-ordinating mark, and can often be used instead of a co-ordinating conjunction like <u>and</u> or <u>but</u>:

> ... in the first 3.0 km of transmission, there is a large lag; then, the wave settles to a steady propagation velocity ...

> ... If heading-reference data are lost, the position-reference data become unusable; the display reacts exactly as if the position-reference data had been lost; after 60 seconds, HEADING DROP OUT is written on the bottom right-hand quadrant of the display.

> ... Engineering works often change the local drainage pattern; changes in the solution rate follow rapidly, with inevitable progressive collapse ...

> ... Time is short; the new plant at X is to be commissioned on April 30th next year; 86 new staff must be recruited and trained before that date ...

> ... Set BATTERY B switch to OFF; set BATTERY C switch to ON.

13.2 Separating items after an 'invoicing' colon

Use semi-colons to separate the items that follow an 'invoicing' colon (a colon that announces that several things are to follow), if the individual items consist of several words:

> ... the responsible manager handles: administration of the basic package; delivery of dumps; transfer of test results; dissemination of modification information.

A short list of individual words is usually best separated simply with commas. For more examples, see the discussion of 'invoicing' colons in section 3.1.

Do NOT use a semi-colon as an 'invoicing' signal. A colon is the correct signal to indicate that a list of items is about to follow. See the discussion of 'invoicing' colons in section 3.1.

Slash (/)

14.1 Signalling 'or'

The slash (sometimes called slant, solidus, oblique, or virgule) signifies an alternative, 'or'; it does NOT signify 'from–to'.

Use slashes sparingly, and use them to express genuine alternatives, such as:

> ... may need adjustment and/or lubrication.

> ... optimized data transmissions may be downloaded/uploaded directly by means of ...

> ... the production of an essay/thesis presents the examiner with ...

Beware of suggesting a false alternative, as in this example:

> During normal/general operation, ...

The use of the slash implies two modes of operation, one called <u>normal</u> and one called <u>general</u>; in fact, the writer is describing only *one* mode of operation, called by alternative names, <u>normal</u> and <u>general</u>. Clearer expression would have been:

> During normal, general operation, ...

> or

> During normal (or 'general') operation, ...

Excessive use of slashes makes a text seem hurried and slapdash. It is usually wiser to use <u>or</u>, not a slash:

... optimized data transmissions may be downloaded or uploaded directly by means of ...

... the production of an essay or thesis presents the examiner with ...

Beware, too, of implying <u>or</u> when you mean <u>and</u>, <u>plus</u>, <u>against</u>, or <u>versus</u>:

... as a test of nuclei quality/performance in the factory
(Better: 'quality and performance' or 'quality against performance')

... adding a water/glycol mixture ...
(The writer intended: 'a mixture of water and glycol')

... any dielectric/electrode combination
(The writer intended: 'combination of dielectric and electrode')

Preferably, do NOT use a slash to express a ratio or a range:

WRITE a water:glycol ratio of ...
    OR a water-to-glycol ratio of ...
  NOT a water/glycol ratio of ...

WRITE a white-to-black range of ...
    OR a white–black range of ...
  NOT a white/black range of ...

14.2 Signalling 'per'

Use a slash to show when a unit for a physical quantity is divided by a unit for another physical quantity:

... m/s = metre(s) per second ...
... rev/min = revolutions per minute ...

14.3 Signalling fractions in prose text

If you wish to include simple fractions in prose text, preferably spell them out in full:

... the thickness can be increased by as much as a quarter.

... using a standard one-tenth-inch grid.

But if the fraction is complex, and would seem clumsy if written out (for example, sixteen two-hundred and fortieths), write it in full-size characters, with a slash separating the numerator from the denominator:

... with a thickness of only 16/240 inch.

... using a standard 1/10 inch grid.

15

Underlining (_)

The most common use for underlining is to emphasise a word in a manuscript or in a typescript produced on a typewriter that has just one typeface. When the manuscript or typescript is printed, the words underlined are italicised:

> ... showed after the significance test that
> the <u>true</u> value was ...
> (becomes 'the *true* value')

> ... note that the <u>relative</u> risk is much
> smaller than ...
> (becomes 'the *relative* risk')

> ... is significant because <u>all</u> sites proved
> more favourable ...
> (becomes 'because *all* sites')

However, underlining can be useful even when you are using a word-processing system that enables you to put text straight into italic type. In this book, for example, I wanted to reserve italic type for giving emphasis to words and phrases in the paragraphs of discussion. That meant I had to find another means of focusing on individual words or phrases taken from my examples. As I explained in the Preface, I decided to set up these conventions:

> For emphasis on words in
> the commentary and discussion: *italic type*

For focusing on words or phrases taken from examples:	<u>underlining</u>
For explaining or defining words that are the subject of discussion in the text:	'inverted commas'

For an example of these conventions in operation, see pages 10 and 11.

A word of warning: do NOT underline long stretches of typescript. Excessive underlining or italicising blurs rather than emphasises the message. To give emphasis to several lines of text, it is usually better to inset those lines, as you would a long quotation.

See also section 10.3 (Inverted Commas) and section 16 (Variations in Printing) for further discussion of means of giving emphasis.

Variations in Printing: Bold Type (as this heading) and Italic Type (*italics*)

16.1 Bolding

Modern electronic equipment has made 'bolding', the use of bold-face type, available to most typists and word-processor operators. Bold-face type can be used effectively to emphasise a word or word-group in continuous text, and can be especially useful to draw attention to difficulties or dangers:

> There are two kinds of macros. Our Month End macro is an example of a **command macro**. ... The other kind of macro is called a **function macro**. This type of macro computes a value ...

> Customers will be seen on a 'first-come, first-served' basis. **No appointments** are to be made for interviews on a Saturday morning, because ...

> Ensure that the correct fuse is fitted in the power-supply fuse-holder (see Section 10 for specifications). **If you are in doubt about making the electrical connections, consult a qualified electrician.**

16.2 The importance of consistency

Be consistent in your use of ways of signalling emphasis. Many modern electronic typewriters and word-processor printers make it possible for you to increase focus on a word or word-group by using five cues, singly or in combination:

- capitalisation;
- inverted commas;

- bolding;

- italics;

- underlining.

Some also allow you to make many changes of type-size and type-style. Preferably, choose just one means of showing a particular type of emphasis, and keep to it. For example, use inverted commas to denote that you are using a word or word-group in an unusual or sceptical way (as described in section 10.3); use italics (underlining in a type-script) to highlight a term or phrase; use bolding only in headings and sub-headings; use capitalisation only as a means of emphasising command names (in computer texts) or proper names. Do not capitalise terms you are using in a general way: you may throw unintended emphasis on those terms (see also section 2).

It is important to control carefully your individual use of print-change cues, because most publishing houses already use variations in type as signals in scientific and technical work. For example, in printed work, vectors and tensors are conventionally distinguished from their scalar equivalents by the use of bold type. In computer documentation, command names are written in full capitals. In biological texts, generic names are printed in italics. If you are producing a text for a scientific context, and your electronic aids make possible a plethora of print-change cues, be sure to conform to the standards established by your professional association and/or your organisation and/or international conventions. Preferably, too, consult a guide to 'do-it-yourself publishing' such as John Miles' *Design for desktop publishing* or a guide to on-line documentation, such as William Horton's *Designing and Writing Online Documentation*. Recognise that, if you have too many print-change cues, you will bewilder rather than help your readers.

16.3 Using italics

Italic type (or underlining in a typescript) can also be used to give emphasis to a word or word-group (see the examples in section 15). Bear in mind, however, the need to establish a consistent system for signalling emphasis, as discussed in 16.2.

Be sparing in the use of italics for emphasis: when too many words are italicised, the emphasis achieved is reduced. Also, when you are writing for on-screen display, recognise that italic type is less easily legible than other fonts, and you may get greater emphasis from bolding, underlining, or use of colour.

Italic type (or underlining in a typescript) is used conventionally by publishing houses to show up the titles of books and journals:

> ... a readable discussion of these points is provided by Colin Cherry in *On Human Communication*, especially in Chapter 3, 'On Signs, Language, and Communication'.

The titles of chapters within books, and of articles within journals, are normally put in inverted commas (see section 10.4).

Italic type (or underlining in a typescript) is used conventionally by publishing houses for *some* foreign words and phrases. Unfortunately, there is no simple rule to follow. For example, *in vivo* and *in vitro* are to be in italic type: in camera is to be in normal print.

Earlier versions of *Hart's Rules* provided a list of words that are to be printed in italics, and another list of words that are to be written in normal print because they are considered 'Anglicised', but *New Hart's Rules* says simply [p123]:

> The best advice is to treat any one item consistently within a given text and follow the newest edition of a suitable dictionary such as *New Oxford Dictionary for Writers and Editors* or the *Shorter Oxford English Dictionary*. Take into account also the subject's conventions and the intended readers' expectations: if in doubt over the degree of assimilation of a particular word, the more cautious policy is to italicize, but in a work written for specialists whose terminology it may be part of, it may be wiser not to.

It is vital that you conform to the conventions of your professional group. In reports of work in the life sciences, you will normally be expected to use italic type (or underlining) for *in vivo* and *in vitro* and all generic names.

However, my principal advice is that you avoid using foreign words and phrases wherever possible. You will not have to debate whether to write *viz.* or viz. (for <u>videlicet</u>) if you use 'namely'. Prefer 'see' to *vide* or *q.v.* (<u>quod vide</u> = 'which see'). Prefer 'face-to-face with' or 'in relation to' or 'as compared with' to *vis-à-vis*, principally because that French expression is now used to carry many different meanings in English text. Prefer 'for example' to e.g., and 'that is' to i.e. (with or without full stops), because many of your readers will be unsure which Latin abbreviation equates to which English phrase.

Part 3

Appendices

Paragraphing

Our awareness of paragraphs in English is due more to their semantic content than to any formal indicators. The most readable prose is the kind that provides for some kind of logical transition at the beginning. The commonest device is the topic sentence. There are hackneyed ways of introducing it – *Next I want to speak of* ...; *We turn now to* ...; *Leaving that for the moment, what can we say of.* ... And sometimes a writer or speaker will number his paragraphs. But as a rule, nothing in particular, least of all syntactic, labels either the beginning or the end.

Dwight Bolinger, *Aspects of Language* [p172]

Reasons for paragraphing

A text must be divided into paragraphs for reasons of logic and emphasis, not just to make it look attractive. The appearance of a text is not *un*important: but primarily, the layout must show how the information is grouped into units of thought or data. In *Modern Rhetoric* [p356], Cleanth Brooks and Robert Penn Warren emphasise the principal function of paragraphing: it enables a writer 'to make his thought structure visible upon the page itself'.

The importance of white space

The thought structure, or pattern of information, is outlined by the white space between paragraphs. Unspaced text is objectionable because it does not signal clearly the boundaries of larger information units on the page, and how those units are patterned. Readers need clear signals to mark the boundaries of larger units like paragraphs just as much as they need signals to mark the boundaries of lower-order units.

But white space also affects the 'attractiveness' of a page. A dense page of type with no white space between paragraphs has a daunting effect. It makes readers feel like tourists who want to climb a tower but are discouraged by a hundred-step staircase with no landings on which to rest and regain breath. Equally, though, a text that consists solely of very short paragraphs is an unattractive prospect: its effect is like that of a hundred-step staircase that has fifty landings separating groups of two steps. We have to find a balance between those two extremes.

The following pages show examples of the extremes. Note the daunting impression created by the text on page 108, which consists entirely of one paragraph. The text on page 109 is also unattractive, even though it is broken into two paragraphs. The practice of omitting line spaces between paragraphs creates a solid, dense impression, which discourages readers even before they start to read the text on the page. The line of white space left between paragraphs is certainly not wasted space: it helps substantially in the process of making thought structure visible.

However, excessive breaking of the text into paragraphs creates a bitty effect, demonstrated by the example on page 110. The example on page 111 shows one way in which the text might be paragraphed more appropriately than in the previous three examples.

Note, too, in all four versions, the uncomfortably varied inter-word spacing created by a poor right-justification system. Well judged and consistent use of white space between paragraphs, between lines, and around text contributes greatly to the readability of a page. Inconsistent amounts of white space, caused by spreading out of words to 'fill' lines, have a disruptive effect. (This is illustrated on pages 108 to 111.)

The linguistic choices made here alter the emphasis and tone of the statements, though the meaning stays the same. The factors that make one or other of the versions more effective as written communication are not matters of accuracy or clarity of technical content, nor are they matters of grammar: they are bound up with the relationship between the writer and the reader(s), and with the context in which the exchange takes place. In other words, in judging effectiveness of communication and suitability of style, we must take into account both the *accuracy* and the *propriety* of the language chosen. If this book is to offer advice on the best style for scientific and technical writing, I must begin by defining the type(s) of writing I have in mind – by defining the writing/reading contexts in which the exchanges are to take place. Only then will it be possible to discuss which tactical choices will best convey the desired meaning with the accuracy, balance, emphasis, and tone required. Broadly, I am concerned with the types of writing that are used for passing scientific and technical information between professional staff in academic, industrial and research organisations: that is, between groups whose intellectual capacities are approximately equal but whose specialist backgrounds may be very different. I am concerned, therefore, with reports, journal articles, proposals, technical memoranda, operating instructions and procedures, specifications, and support documentation for equipment. I am not suggesting tactics for explaining complex scientific and technical ideas to the general public. Mass communication poses special problems of selection and presentation, which are not the concern of the average engineer or scientist. Nor am I suggesting tactics for advertising and commercial writing. Though *all* communication is in a sense an attempt to sell someone else our ideas, there is a difference in degree between the tactics needed to advocate a change from one soap powder to another, and those needed to present new scientific ideas to colleagues in industry and research. I am concerned with the main writing tasks that confront professional ...

A page illustrating the daunting impression
created by a very long paragraph

The linguistic choices made here alter the emphasis and tone of the statements, though the meaning stays the same. The factors that make one or other of the versions more effective as written communication are not matters of accuracy or clarity of technical content, nor are they matters of grammar: they are bound up with the relationship between the writer and the reader(s), and with the context in which the exchange takes place. In other words, in judging effectiveness of communication and suitability of style, we must take into account both the *accuracy* and the *propriety* of the language chosen. If this book is to offer advice on the best style for scientific and technical writing, I must begin by defining the type(s) of writing I have in mind – by defining the writing/reading contexts in which the exchanges are to take place. Only then will it be possible to discuss which tactical choices will best convey the desired meaning with the accuracy, balance, emphasis, and tone required.

Broadly, I am concerned with the types of writing that are used for passing scientific and technical information between professional staff in academic, industrial and research organisations: that is, between groups whose intellectual capacities are approximately equal but whose specialist backgrounds may be very different. I am concerned, therefore, with reports, journal articles, proposals, technical memoranda, operating instructions and procedures, specifications, and support documentation for equipment. I am not suggesting tactics for explaining complex scientific and technical ideas to the general public. Mass communication poses special problems of selection and presentation, which are not the concern of the average engineer or scientist. Nor am I suggesting tactics for advertising and commercial writing. Though *all* communication is in a sense an attempt to sell someone else our ideas, there is a difference in degree between the tactics needed to advocate a change from one soap powder to another, and those needed to present new scientific ideas to colleagues in industry and research. I am . . .

A page illustrating the dense impression created
by omission of line spaces between paragraph

The linguistic choices made here alter the emphasis and tone of the statements, though the meaning stays the same.

The factors that make one or other of the versions more effective as written communication are not matters of accuracy or clarity of technical content, nor are they matters of grammar: they are bound up with the relationship between the writer and the reader(s), and with the context in which the exchange takes place.

In other words, in judging effectiveness of communication and suitability of style, we must take into account both the *accuracy* and the *propriety* of the language chosen.

If this book is to offer advice on the best style for scientific and technical writing, I must begin by defining the type(s) of writing I have in mind – by defining the writing/reading contexts in which the exchanges are to take place. Only then will it be possible to discuss which tactical choices will best convey the desired meaning with the accuracy, balance, emphasis, and tone required.

Broadly, I am concerned with the types of writing that are used for passing scientific and technical information between professional staff in academic, industrial and research organisations: that is, between groups whose intellectual capacities are approximately equal but whose specialist backgrounds may be very different.

I am concerned, therefore, with reports, journal articles, proposals, technical memoranda, operating instructions and procedures, specifications, and support documentation for equipment.

I am not suggesting tactics for explaining complex scientific and technical ideas to the general public. Mass communication poses special problems of selection and presentation, which are not the concern of the average engineer or scientist. Nor am I suggesting ...

A page illustrating the bitty effect
created by excessive division into paragraphs

The linguistic choices made here alter the emphasis and tone of the statements, though the meaning stays the same.

The factors that make one or other of the versions more effective as written communication are not matters of accuracy or clarity of technical content, nor are they matters of grammar: they are bound up with the relationship between the writer and the reader(s), and with the context in which the exchange takes place. In other words, in judging effectiveness of communication and suitability of style, we must take into account both the *accuracy* and the *propriety* of the language chosen.

If this book is to offer advice on the best style for scientific and technical writing, I must begin by defining the type(s) of writing I have in mind – by defining the writing/reading contexts in which the exchanges are to take place. Only then will it be possible to discuss which tactical choices will best convey the desired meaning with the accuracy, balance, emphasis, and tone required.

Broadly, I am concerned with the types of writing that are used for passing scientific and technical information between professional staff in academic, industrial and research organisations: that is, between groups whose intellectual capacities are approximately equal but whose specialist backgrounds may be very different. I am concerned, therefore, with reports, journal articles, proposals, technical memoranda, operating instructions and procedures, specifications, and support documentation for equipment.

I am not suggesting tactics for explaining complex scientific and technical ideas to the general public. Mass communication poses special problems of selection and presentation, which are not the concern of the average engineer or scientist. Nor am I suggesting tactics for advertising and commercial writing. Though *all* communication is in a sense an attempt to sell someone else our ideas, there is a difference in degree between the tactics needed to ...

One way in which the text might be paragraphed more appropriately than in the previous three example pages

Length of paragraphs

There is no formula by which either the length or the structure of a paragraph can be judged as 'good' or 'bad'. In *A Comprehensive Grammar of the English Language* [p1624], Professor Randolph Quirk and his colleagues say:

> Rather than attempting to recommend an ideal size of paragraph or models for its ideal identity, we should note that the paragraph enables a writer to show that a particular set of sentences should be considered as more closely related to each other, and that those grouped within one paragraph are to be seen as a whole in relation to those that are grouped in the paragraphs preceding and following.

A paragraph should deal with only one topic: but to explain everything about one topic, you may need several paragraphs, each consisting of a group of related points. A topic may therefore be covered in one single-sentence paragraph or in a sequence of paragraphs that all contain several sentences.

Rough 'rules of thumb' for length are:

* single-sentence paragraphs should appear only rarely, to give special emphasis to a topic or point;

* paragraphs covering more than one-third of a page will probably overwhelm your reader.

Links and opening sentences

A well written paragraph will normally announce its topic in its opening sentence, and go on to develop that topic – give additional facts or discuss particular aspects – in succeeding sentences. Well written text also makes ample use of link words and link phrases to signal to readers the relationship between information in the new paragraph and information they have just absorbed:

> As a result, ...
> At the same time, ...
> In contrast, ...
> For the same reason, ...

So, ...
Accordingly, ...

However, beware of giving your work the 'hackneyed' tone mentioned by Bolinger on page 105.

Review your writing for coherence and emphasis. To review coherence, look to see if your ideas are in a clear, logical order, comfortably packed together. To check emphasis, look to see if the main things you want to say are prominent, either in short paragraphs on their own or in dominant positions in longer paragraphs (dominant positions are the beginnings and ends). Look for *variety* of structure: if all your paragraphs are much the same structure and length, look for an opportunity to emphasise the main topics by re-structuring your text.

Word-Division

The main principle ... is that the word division should be as unobtrusive as possible, so that the reader continues reading without faltering or momentary confusion.

New Hart's Rules [p59]

Word-division is a matter of layout, not punctuation; but it is closely related to punctuation, because it requires the use of a signal, a hyphen, to help readers find their way quickly and confidently along the lines of written words.

Since word-division is essentially the breaking of a customary signal (a word) into two parts, it is inevitably disruptive to the reader's concentration. It is desirable, therefore, to avoid it as much as possible. Where it is unavoidable, use the following guidelines.

Divide according to etymology, where the etymology is obvious:

fluor-escent	manu-facture
bio-logical	tele-phone
de-stabilise	trans-port
hydro-chloric	verifi-able

If division according to etymology is not possible, divide according to pronunciation or syllabification. Where possible, break the word where two consonants come together. If there is only one consonant at the suitable break-boundary, normally take that consonant to begin the second line, unless etymology dictates otherwise. Also, where the single consonant precedes a common suffix, the consonant is not normally taken over on to the next line:

ac-tive	quan-tity
bal-ance	read-ings
cali-bration	severe-ly
cre-ated	se-verely
fail-ure	stag-nant
oc-curring	thick-ness
prob-able	truth-fully
pump-ing	vi-able

Note that division between vowels is permitted, *provided* that they are sounded separately, as in <u>cre-ated</u> and <u>vi-able</u>.

Writers for whom English is a foreign language may find it useful to refer for guidance to the *Oxford Advanced Learner's Dictionary of Current English*, which indicates where words may be broken.

Do not divide single-syllable words such as <u>small</u>, <u>old</u>, <u>climb</u>; preferably, do not divide short two-syllable words like <u>over, easy, limit</u>.

Do not divide a word in a way that would leave just one letter at the beginning or end of a word: for example, keep words like <u>apart</u>, <u>epoxy</u>, <u>patchy</u> and <u>cloudy</u> unbroken.

Where two consonants together form one sound, as in <u>climbing</u>, do not divide the consonants: write <u>climb-ing</u>, <u>with-in</u>, <u>tech-nology</u> (NOT tec-hnology).

If a word has a final consonant that is doubled before an <u>-ing</u> ending, take the added consonant to begin the next line:

bud-ding	fit-ting
crop-ping	set-ting

Similarly, take over the added consonant when the final consonant is added before an <u>-ed</u> ending:

WRITE bud-ded	NOT budd-ed
fit-ted	fitt-ed

Wherever possible, however, write words such as <u>budding</u> and <u>fitted</u> in full. This is especially important when the word would normally be pronounced as a single syllable: <u>cropped</u>, <u>strapped</u>.

Do not divide words at an <u>-ed</u> ending that indicates a past tense; write the word in full, or with a break earlier in the word:

ab-sorbed	missed
charged	noted
closed	pro-jected
de-pended	re-vealed

In general, avoid any word-division that would leave only two letters after the break (although in modern practice, words ending in <u>-ly</u> are often broken before that suffix).

If a word is hyphenated already, break the word at the hyphen; never introduce a second hyphen.

Do not divide numbers at line-ends, and do not separate abbreviated units from their numbers. For example, do not write <u>6</u> at the end of one line, and <u>g</u> (for grammes) at the beginning of the next.

Preferably, do not divide personal names; but if you have to do so, follow normal rules of division in full names like Richard or Kirkman.

If you are using just an initial letter to represent a single first name, do not divide between the initial and the surname. If you are using two or more initials to represent first names, and if division is unavoidable, divide between the initials and the surname.

Avoid dividing words in ways that would leave confusing elements at line-ends, such as <u>the-ory</u>, <u>an-ticipated</u>, or <u>can-celled</u>.

If possible, never end a page with a divided word.

Finally, a helpful warning from the *The Cambridge Guide to English Usage* [p582]:

> The computer's automatic wordbreaking system can be set to execute some of these principles, but the output still needs an editorial eye to check for infelicities.

Differences in Punctuation in American English and British English

In preparing this appendix, I have had the generous help of Jean and Richard Chisholm (Richard Chisholm was formerly Chair of the Department of English, Plymouth State College of the University System of New Hampshire).

The notes in this appendix relate only to the main aspects of punctuation that affect technical writing and editing in the USA. We do not attempt to cover punctuation for non-technical writing (though there are few differences of principle). For detailed guidance on points not discussed in this book (such as punctuation in correspondence), see *The Chicago Manual of Style* or *Merriam-Webster's Manual for Writers and Editors*.

Conventions

Abbreviations

In these notes, for the sake of brevity, we use the following abbreviations:

AE	American English
BE	British English
Chicago	*The Chicago Manual of Style*, University of Chicago Press, 15th Edition 2003
Webster	*Merriam-Webster's Standard American Style Manual*, Merriam-Webster, 1998

Page references

The page references after each side-heading in these notes are to the pages in Part 2 in which the British usage of the mark concerned is discussed.

Note

In general, only *differences* between American conventions and British conventions are discussed in these notes. Where there is no note about a mark (for instance, about the use of dashes or ellipsis points), AE and BE usage are for all practical purposes identical.

Notes on the Differences in Punctuation in American English and British English

APOSTROPHE (pages 21–23)

Chicago agrees [p281] with the general BE convention that the plural of single letters, acronyms, and numbers should usually be formed by the simple addition of *s*; but it suggests that apostrophes should be used to form the plurals of abbreviations with periods, of lower-case letters, and of capital letters that might be confusing if <u>s</u> alone were added. For example:

Ph.D.'s   *x*'s and *y*'s   A's, I's, S's

COLON (pages 27–33)

Colon to introduce lists

The various ways of punctuating lists in BE are all current also in AE. *Chicago* [p272] declares that an 'invoicing' colon (a colon introducing a list of items to follow) should normally be preceded by a grammatically complete sentence such as:

> As a general guide, the manual should be specified in some detail if one of the following conditions applies:
>
> 1) the client has little experience in that field of operation ...

rather than:

> As a general guide, the manual should be specified in some detail if:
>
> 1) the client has little experience in that field of operation ...

But practice in the USA is changing. The following incomplete sentences, all followed by bulleted or numbered lists, are from documentation by major American companies whose standards of technical writing are high:

> Accordingly, they are preferred for conditions such as where:
> (Du Pont)

> On some systems, however, this may not work, and you'll see the message:
> (Hewlett-Packard)

> If you can't find the name of a macro you want in the appropriate dialog box listing:
> (Microsoft)

> To select the downloaded font:
> (IBM)

And the following are from books by major American publishing houses:

> Some of the issues that need to be addressed are:
> (Ablex)

> To solve both problems you need to use:
> (Xerox Press)

> The file contains:
> (Microsoft Press)

> Methods of blinking include alternating between:
> (Wiley)

> Identifiable techniques include:
> (Addison Wesley)

BE does not usually omit the 'invoicing' colon above a list, but in AE, the colon is often omitted:

> The usual ones are
>
> > "Hold" points during fabrication
> > Performance tests
> > Shipping

Receiving
Installation

Additional features include

- Paragraph numbering
- Comparing two versions of a document
- Sorting and calculating information in documents
- Repaginating documents

British writers producing texts for the American market should be aware that editors in the USA may wish to change the use of colons before displayed lists in a BE draft; but it is likely nowadays that BE usage of invoicing colons will pass unaltered by editors, and will not confuse AE readers.

Invoicing colons in continuous text (introducing a 'run-in' list) should preferably be preceded by a complete sentence, according to *Chicago* [p271], as in:

The game has three modes of operation: Attract, Play, and Self-Test.

There are two file types that you can use to store data: ABC and DEF.

But again, AE practice is changing, and use of an incomplete sentence before a colon is not uncommon:

Proof functions performed are: full field encoding, endorsing, bank stamp printing, recording on microfilm, accumulating totals, lister printouts, and sorting of documents.

Chicago specifies [p271] that numerals or letters that mark divisions in a run-in list should be enclosed in parentheses. In BE, it would be usual to precede a run-in list with a colon, irrespective of the structure immediately before the list. Chicago says:

No punctuation precedes the first parenthesis if the last word of the introductory material is a verb or preposition. If the introductory material is an independent clause, a colon should precede the first parenthesis.

Webster says [p102]:

> The entire list is introduced by a colon if it is preceded by a full clause, and often when it is not.

Both authorities recommend that, if the ensuing list is long, and if each item within the list consists of several words, the list should be set as a display.

Colon within a sentence, separating clauses

In both BE and AE, writers use a colon in a continuous sentence to introduce supplementary, enlarging, or antithetical information. For example:

> Writing a card's goal statement often involves translating system jargon that appeared in menus and messages into ordinary language: the jargon should go.

> Thus, in one sense, the plan was an effective transactional document: it motivated individuals to act in ways that helped establish the organization.

> ABC adopts a descriptive approach: each of the disorders is defined with specific operational criteria which are either observable or verifiable clinical findings.

> This raises a problem for documentation designers: the choice between photographs and drawings to represent an object.

However, AE writers are more likely to use a semicolon before a second clause that illustrates or amplifies the first:

> Even within the computer industry, usability/acceptance testing is still almost exclusively after the fact of production; there is rarely time in the development cycle for major problems identified in feedback to be changed.

> X points out a problem with the administration of the pretest; a pretest can "sensitize" the treatment group to perform differently on the posttest.

Pressing the LOCAL key will temporarily stop the mode; pressing the ABC or DEF key will start it again.

For light work, use tools that work well with brass; for filled compositions, use carbide-tipped tools.

A and B offer a useful alternative contrast between browsing and navigation; the former deals predominately with internal links in a document, the latter mainly with external links.

Once again, British writers producing a text for the AE market can expect that some editors in the USA will change BE usage, but that many will let it stand. It is unlikely that the BE usage will confuse AE readers. BE readers, however, may well be surprised by the AE use of a semicolon before an amplifying second clause.

For more discussion of AE use of semicolons, see page 135.

Capitalisation after colons

In BE, a colon in continuous text should always be followed by a lower-case letter. The only exception might seem to be when the colon precedes a quotation, but in those circumstances the colon is actually followed by an inverted comma, to indicate the special status of the words that follow.

In AE, the first word after a colon in continuous text is sometimes started with a capital letter. Usually, the first word after a colon begins with a lower-case letter, but if the text after the colon is a complete sentence (especially if it is a long sentence), writers often start the first word with a capital letter:

These representations can be made subject to transformation and procedures of various kinds: They can be rotated, enlarged, or reduced ...

Just remember: It takes a little more time to make a command easy to use, but the investment is usually worthwhile especially if someone other than you will use the command.

But you should be extremely careful when doing this: Be sure you don't accidentally remove files that you needed.

Webster sums up the choice for AE writers as follows [p37]:

> The first word following a colon is lowercased when it begins a list and usually lowercased when it begins a complete sentence. However, when the sentence introduced is lengthy and distinctly separate from the preceding clause, it is often capitalized. If a colon introduces a series of sentences, the first word of each sentence is capitalized.

Colon after the salutation in a letter

In the USA, a colon is used after the salutation in a formal letter:

Dear Mr. Brown: Ladies and Gentlemen:

but in informal correspondence, a comma takes the place of a colon:

Dear Albert,

COMMA (pages 34–52)

Comma before and

In discussing the use of commas within sentences, authorities in the USA urge writers to follow different conventions in different sentence structures. Writers should distinguish between a compound sentence (two or more independent clauses) and a sentence that has a compound predicate (two or more verbs that relate to the same subject).

A 'compound sentence' is a sentence structure in which two complete clauses, each with its own subject, are co-ordinated into a single statement. A comma *is* used before the and or other conjunction co-ordinating the two clauses:

The main standards give test methods,
and
the appendices specify minimum values.

Items serve as the nodes of the knowledge network,
and
user-defined relators serve as the links between items.

The difference between the speeds of the lowering bands is fixed
by pre-set resistors in the relay-coil circuit,
and
their relative displacement is non-adjustable.

A 'sentence that has a compound predicate' is one in which a single subject is followed by two linked phrases. Normally, *no* comma is used before the co-ordinating <u>and</u> or other conjunction:

	shows you the size of each file
ABC	and
	gives you the date and the time the file was created.

	is intended especially for architectural and acoustic investigations
The weighting	and
	facilitates recording of sound-pressure decay curves for determination of reverberation time.

	mimics the situation in a normal developer tray when coated donor and receiver are processed
This	and
	represents an extreme akin to a high-exposure region on a donor ...

Webster says [p7–8]:

Commas are not normally used to separate the parts of a compound predicate. ...

but adds a note:

However, they are often used if the predicate is long and complicated, if one part is being stressed, or if the absence of a comma could cause a momentary misreading.

The following examples from AE writing illustrate *Webster*'s note:

The DNA sequences of the $_H$ genes from the Reed-Sternberg cells were potentially translatable into proteins, and were thus functional.

The six bytes that follow the function code are not specified by the ABC driver, and may be used by the system program to transfer communication and control information to the satellite program

Textual modifications are shown immediately to the person who initiates them, but are indicated on other users' screens by the appearance of "clouds" over the original text.

It seems, therefore, that modern practice in AE is much the same as the BE practice described in section 4.7 (pages 46–51): to omit commas when the items co-ordinated by <u>and</u> are short and manageable, and no ambiguity is likely; and, irrespective of the grammar of the sentence, to insert commas if doing so will help make clear the logic, balance, or emphasis required. Nevertheless, British writers producing a draft text for the AE market should not be surprised if an AE editor changes the draft to conform to AE usage.

Commas in numbers

In the USA, authorities on punctuation usually recommend use of commas to separate numbers that consist of four digits or more (that is, writers should write 9,850 units, or $75,000.00, or 12,345.6). However, exceptions are recommended for scientific work or for texts that are to be distributed internationally.

The international standard ISO31/0: Part 0, *Specification for quantities, units and symbols*, is unequivocal about how numbers should be set [p11]:

> To facilitate the reading of numbers with many digits, these may be separated into suitable groups, preferably of three, counting from the decimal sign towards the left and the right; the groups should be separated by a small space and never by a comma, a point, nor by other means.

Unfortunately, the acceptance of metrication and the conventions of the International System of Units (SI Units) has been even slower in the USA than in Britain, and common practice is still to use commas. It is wise, if you have a suitable opportunity to do so, to explain in a preface or foreword the conventions you are following. Certainly, all writers within an organisation should use the same conventions consistently.

Comma as a decimal point

In AE, a decimal point is usually expressed by a period (full stop), not by a comma.

Commas in an address

In *Postal Addressing Standards, Publication 28*, the US Postal Service states the following preference for layout of a displayed address:

Mr James Jones
4417 Brook St NE
Washington DC 20019–4649

FULL STOP/PERIOD (pages 62–65)

A full stop is generally called a period in AE. Its use is virtually the same in AE as in BE. One difference is the placing of a period in relation to inverted commas (quotation marks) and parentheses. For a discussion of the differences of usage in AE and BE, see the sections on inverted commas (quotation marks) (pages 78–83) and parentheses (pages 84–88).

Also, AE writers use periods after abbreviations more frequently than is common in BE usage. In writing abbreviations, BE practice is to use stops only after true abbreviations (truncations), in which the end of the word is removed. When an abbreviation is formed by the removal of the interior of the word, no stop is used. Common AE usage is to put a stop after true abbreviations *and* after words from which the interior has been removed. *Webster* [p80] says:

A period follows most abbreviations that are formed by omitting letters from the middle of a word

(such as *amt*. for 'amount' or *Dr*. for 'Doctor') but also says [p79]:

The contemporary styling of abbreviations is inconsistent and arbitrary, and no set of rules can hope to cover all the possible variations, exceptions, and peculiarities encountered in print. ... In doubtful cases, a good general dictionary or a dictionary of abbreviations will usually show standard forms for common abbreviations.

It seems necessary, therefore, to learn an arbitrary list of different usages. The style guides of many large companies contain such lists. *Chicago* [p571–592] provides a lengthy discussion, with lists, of scholarly abbreviations, including many from technology and science.

Two points are worth stressing:

1. No periods are used after any of the SI abbreviations, and the same abbreviations are used for both the singular and the plural.

2. Within acronyms (single words formed from the initial letters of several words), no periods are used:

ANSI   ASCII   COBOL   RAM   ROM

HYPHEN (pages 66–77)

AE writers spell words solid more frequently and sooner than BE writers. Many, though by no means all, BE writers keep hyphens in well established words like co-operative, co-ordination, re-license, and re-live, and are slow to join up new coinages like workstation, widebody, or throughput. AE writers, following authorities such as *Chicago*, write them solid sooner, and create permanent compounds. *Chicago* acknowledges that there is wide variety in AE usage, and emphasises [p299] that the first place to look for answers is the dictionary. However, *Webster* warns [p67] that a dictionary may not always supply you with an answer:

> A good dictionary will list many *permanent compounds*, compounds so commonly used that they have become permanent parts of the language. It will not list *temporary compounds*, those created to meet a writer's need at a particular moment. ... Writers thus cannot rely wholly on dictionaries to guide them in writing compounds.

In general, rules for forming temporary compounds in AE are as in BE. For AE usage on word-division, see pages 135–137.

INVERTED COMMAS (QUOTATION MARKS)
(pages 78–83)

In the USA, the term *quotation marks* is used instead of *inverted commas*. Indeed, many (perhaps most) AE readers would be nonplussed by the BE term.

Showing quotations within quotations

AE writers use double inverted commas as the norm to set off direct quotations, and use single marks for quotations within quotations:

> ... seek to enjoin these Federal departments from authorizing, approxing, or funding any programs that "contribute to the 'greenhouse effect'" until ...

> "When technical documentation managers and software technical writers are asked to identify the biggest problem area they have on the job, they respond unanimously 'Getting information from developers.'"

Placing other marks with inverted commas

AE writers put periods and commas inside inverted commas (to use the terms of the discussion on pages 80–81, they punctuate for neatness, not for logic). However, they put colons and semi-colons outside inverted commas:

> ... waits for you to enter any of several commands that say, in effect, "Edlin, do this to my file."

> PLATO is an acronym for "Programmed Learning for Automatic Teaching Operations."

> The term "population," used to some extent in qualitative research, is ...

> ... you may decide to add a "wrapper": add an introduction and ...

> ... asked her to select an item from a "list-box"; when she looked ...

> ... writing and editing cycles belong to the "nonrationalized domains of most industrial operations"; that ...

AE writers put question marks, exclamation marks, and dashes inside or outside inverted commas, depending on whether the extra marks relate only to the quotation or to the whole sentence:

> Is this part of the "core"?

> To paraphrase the response of many to this circumstance, "why would anybody want to *do* that?"

> For example, learners would complete exercises and exclaim, "I know we did something, but I don't know what it is!".

> Another way is to "pass the baton" – make a single ...

Where three marks should theoretically come together (as in the middle two examples immediately above), sometimes AE writers omit the final full stop (as in the second of the examples above).

Using inverted commas to highlight

AE writers use inverted commas in the same ways as BE writers to highlight new terms, to focus on a formal name or label, to emphasise that a word is being used in an unusual or special way, or to encourage readers to learn key terms:

> ... what the company called a "significant" new field ...

> This is a "widening step," ...

> ... users know what constitutes a "system fatal error" ...

> X Company, for example, has no "small" stores.

> Before 1988, "proved" reserves included ...

> This results in a large number of "lists" in a short travel distance.

> ... population comparisons were made by use of a "basal" subset of cases ...

In general, however, AE writers use quotation marks for highlighting less frequently than BE writers. Especially, use of quotation marks for rhetorical effect – to indicate irony or special colour – is less frequent. In general, too, as in Britain, now that word-processing equipment is widely available, AE writers increasingly use italics or bold to highlight terms:

... is called a *datagram* and is contained in a *packet* ...

... to reduce its load on the channel (*backing off*).

... bit-mapped graphics allow independent *windows* that can be overlapped ...

... intended for a single vendor will be termed a *simple specification.*

... a border with eight boxes (called *handles*) ...

PARENTHESES (pages 84–88)

In using parentheses and brackets for enclosure (as 'signs of aggregation', commonly called *fences* [*Webster* p113; *Chicago* p535]) in mathematical work, *Chicago* and *Webster* agree with *Copy-Editing* (Cambridge University Press) and *New Hart's Rules* (Oxford University Press) that the sequence should be:

$$\{[(.....)]\}$$

However, the use of parentheses and brackets as part of mathematical or scientific nomenclature is a complex topic, and as stated in the Preface and on page 85, you should be sure to conform to the conventions established in your science or technology.

If some material in parentheses is included at the end of a sentence, AE practice and BE practice are the same – to put the full stop (period) or question mark that marks the end of the sentence outside the parentheses:

... or a specialized format (defined by the user with IMAGE statements).

Are they self-contained entities that could be transported to other publications (without their links to the current publication)?

If the text within parentheses is a complete sentence, AE and BE punctuation are again the same – to place the full stop or other mark belonging to that complete sentence within the parentheses. No stop is needed outside the parentheses:

... the fault of the manual. (Note, further, that this interface is supposed to be so friendly that one does not need to use the manual!) Further complicating ...

... constitutes part of the Nation's domestic energy supply. (See Introduction, page 1.) Federal offshore ...

... either a node address or an adjacency. (An adjacency is used for loopback testing under the control of Network Management.) The table enables the ...

A comma marking a word-group within a sentence is placed *outside* parentheses, not *inside* as it is for inverted commas (quotation marks):

Wind power classes are based on the average "wind power density," expressed in watts per square meter (W/m²), which incorporates ...

If the new status is "standby" or "not operating," it is handled separately (by operator action), and has no ...

A semi-colon or colon marking a word-group within a sentence is placed *outside* parentheses:

... transmission errors (either A or B status characters); and an extra ...

Vannevar Bush's conjectures on this area have been borne out remarkably accurately (although he believed the medium would be microfilm): "The Encyclopaedia Britannica ...

PERIOD: see FULL STOP

QUOTATION MARKS: see INVERTED COMMAS

SEMI-COLON (pages 91–92)

In AE usage, <u>semicolon</u> is usually written without a hyphen.

As discussed in the section on colons (page 121) AE writers use fewer 'enlarging' colons (colons used within sentences in which the second part enlarges on the statement made in the first part) than BE writers. For example, in the following AE sentences, BE writers would probably have used colons, not semi-colons:

... problems are not given; they must be analyzed and posited in an answerable form before ...

Don't worry; the real text comes at the beginning of the next chapter.

Carbide tooling is recommended; usually a C-2 grade is adequate.

However, BE writers are unlikely to find that an AE editor will change an 'enlarging' colon into a semi-colon.

WORD-DIVISION (pages 115–118)

The general principle of word-division preferred by *Chicago* [p287] is to divide in accordance with pronunciation rather than derivation. In BE, word-division is based on a combination of etymology and syllabification or pronunciation.

On both sides of the Atlantic, wide variations are permitted. *Chicago* [p693] advises AE writers to follow the guidance given in *Merriam-Webster's Collegiate Dictionary*, which includes in its entry for each word suggestions for where that word might be broken. However, for most words, *several* division-points are suggested.

For example, the *Merriam-Webster Collegiate Dictionary* suggests [p11a] that pos/si/bil/i/ty might be divided in any of the following ways:

```
pos-      sibility
possi-    bility
possibil-      ity
possibili-     ty
```

BE writers can find similar guidance in *The Oxford Advanced Learner's Dictionary of Current English*. That dictionary, too, suggests [p661] alternative divisions for possibility, though a shorter list than in AE:

```
possi-    bility
possibil-      ity
```

Differences in pronunciation, not only between AE and BE but also within AE and BE, lead to varying interpretations of where syllables begin and end. As *Webster's New Collegiate Dictionary* says [p11a]:

It is ... all but impossible to produce a convincing argument that either of the divisions aus/ter/i/ty, au/ster/i/ty is better than the other.

Accordingly, it is not possible to state with confidence how an AE editor might revise a draft BE text.

Though BE writers and readers might find the AE divisions unusual, it is unlikely that they would find them confusing. Similarly, AE writers and readers might notice differences in BE practice, but would probably not be confused by them. So, conform consistently to one general principle, but be prepared for an editor 'on the other side' to change some of your word-divisions.

Fortunately, the list of *unacceptable* word-divisions is the same in both AE and BE (for examples to illustrate the following reminders, see pages 116–118).

- Do not divide single-syllable words.

- Do not divide a word in a way that would leave just one letter at the beginning or end of a line.

- If possible, divide a word where two consonants come together, but do not separate the consonants if they are pronounced as a single sound (write <u>foun/dation</u> but not <u>backtrac/king</u>).

- Divide between vowels only if the two vowels are pronounced separately (as in <u>cre/ated</u>).

- Do not divide words before an <u>-ed</u> ending that indicates a past tense; and generally avoid any word-division that would leave only two letters after the break.

- Do not divide word-endings such as <u>-tion</u>, <u>-tial</u>, <u>-able</u>, <u>-ible-</u>, <u>-ial</u>, and <u>-tious</u>.

- If a word has a doubled consonant before an <u>-ing</u> or <u>-ed</u> ending, take one consonant to the next line (write <u>bud/ded</u> and <u>fit/ting</u> not <u>budd/ed</u> and <u>fitt/ing</u>).

- If a word is hyphenated already, divide it at the hyphen; do not introduce a second hyphen.

- Do not divide numbers at line-ends, and do not separate abbreviated units from their numbers.

- Try not to divide names, if possible.

- Avoid dividing words in ways that would leave confusing elements at line-ends.

Bibliography

A Comprehensive Grammar of the English Language, Quirk R., Greenbaum S., Leech G., and Svartvik J., Longman, Harlow, Essex, 1985

Aspects of Language, Bolinger D., Harcourt Brace Jovanovich, New York, 1975

British Standard 5775: Part 0: 1993, Specification for quantities, units and symbols, British Standards Institution, London, 1993 (identical with International Organization for Standardization ISO 31–0: 1992)

Collins Cobuild English Grammar, Second Edition, Harper Collins, Glasgow, 2005

Collins Cobuild English Usage, Second Edition, Harper Collins, Glasgow, 2004

Copy-Editing: the Cambridge handbook, Third Edition, Butcher J., Cambridge University Press, Cambridge, 1992

Design for Desktop Publishing, Miles J., Gordon Fraser, London, 1987

Designing and Writing Online Documentation, Horton W., Wiley, New York, 1990

Guide to Effective Software Technical Writing, Browning C., Prentice-Hall, Englewood Cliffs, New Jersey, 1984

How to Write Metric, Metrication Board, HMSO, London, 1978

ISO 31–0: 1992: see British Standard 5775.

Merriam-Webster's Collegiate Dictionary, 11th Edition, Merriam-Webster, Springfield, Massachusetts, 2003

Merriam-Webster's Manual for Writers and Editors, Merriam-Webster, Springfield, Massachusetts, 1998

Mind the Stop, Carey G. V., Penguin, Harmondsworth, 1986

Modern English Usage, Fowler H. W., Second Edition revised by Sir Ernest Gowers, Oxford University Press, Oxford, 1965

Modern Rhetoric, Brooks C., and Warren R. P., Harcourt Brace Jovanovich, 1970

New Hart's Rules: the Handbook of Style for Writers and Editors, Oxford University Press, Oxford, 2005

New Oxford Dictionary for Writers and Editors, Oxford University Press, Oxford, 2005

Oxford Advanced Learner's Dictionary of Current English, Third Edition, Hornby A.S., Oxford University Press, Oxford, 1974

Postal Addressing Standards, Publication 28, US Postal Service website, Postal Explorer, 'Properly formatted mailpiece'

The Cambridge Guide to English Usage, Peters P., Cambridge University Press, Cambridge, 2004

The Chicago Manual of Style, 15th Edition, University of Chicago Press, London, 2003

The Economist Style Guide, Ninth Edition, Profile Books, London, 2005

The King's English, Third Edition, Fowler H. W. and E. G., Oxford University Press, Oxford, 1930

The Oxford Guide to Style, Ritter R. M., Oxford University Press, Oxford, 2002

You Have a Point There, Partridge E., Routledge and Kegan Paul, London, 1983

Index